Nov. 23, 1993

DO YOU NEED
A MIRACLE?

by
Ann Brown

To the Palo Duro Church
Library.
May this little book
help you find the
miracles you need.

Ann Brown

Spirit Press & Publication
Del City, Oklahoma

DO YOU NEED A MIRACLE?

Printed by Spirit Press & Publications
P.O. Box 15742
Del City, OK 73155-5742

by Ann Brown

DEDICATION TO

Laura Lokey Walker, my beloved mother, who brought me up "in the nurture and admontion of the Lord."

ACKNOWLEDGEMENTS

I'm grateful to my many Bible and psychology teachers, especially Georgia Bussell Watson, Dr. John W. Cobb, Dr. Fred D. Howard, Dr. John A Freeman, and Dr. Murray R. Kovnar, but most of all to the Master Teacher who inspired me to write this book.

FOREWORD

As I pursued the subjects discussed in this manuscript *Do You Need a Miracle?*, I was persuaded at once what Ann Brown had written deserved more than a casual reading. Her first book published, *Scarlet Thread*, a scholarly dissertation on the life and death of Jesus Christ, was well received by the public, and especially by those who believe in Christ as their personal Savior. In fact, the book has been sold out for some time. She has had the one book published, and four more seeking a publisher. God grant they all will be published. Our world needs all of that which this author has written.

With the skill of her craft, the life experience of faithfully serving God, and her keen expertise in Christian counseling, ANN BROWN has written a Biblically researched "how to" for home and family; health and vocation; God and church.

The result of her spirit-led writing provides an educational study of Christian ethic, and a timeless , spaceless solution to the moral sickness of our world.

With an easy flowing structure of personal comments, dialogue-type questions and answers, ANN BROWN covers all the bases of God's plan for man's happiness on this earth and the life hereafter.

From her compilation of cause and effect, you find the golden rules of how to choose a mate: marital problems; what to do with rebellious children; your work; your health; and your pursuit of happiness.

There are several gems of philosophy like: "Chasing wealth is much like a dog chasing his tail: If he catches it, what has he accomplished?"

"Henry Ford's formula for a happy marriage was the same one he used to make a successful car: 'Stick to one model'."

In marriage: "It is wiser to spend more time making over him than making him over."

In this book, which combines Biblical scripture references and author comments about day-to-day challenges of life's social changes, ANN BROWN provides the answers to questions we all express silently if not publicly. She concludes miracles in life are still possible - if we follow God's instructions. "And they are ample from Genesis to The Revelation."

ANN BROWN is a veteran homemaker. She has been married to a farmer-rancher for 57 years, and is the mother of two sons, and many foster daughters. The elder son, Dr. Gilbert C. Brown, Jr. is a research psychologist at Brooks Aero-Space Medical Laboratory in San Antonio, Texas. Dr. Dean Brown is a family physician in Amarillo, Texas. The daughters are scattered all over the United States. The Browns have four grandsons.

Mrs. Brown for 25 years was a full-time wife and mother. Then she went back to college as a second-semester freshman in September of 1959. She graduated Cum Laude from Wayland Baptist College in May, 1961, with majors in English and psychology, and a minor in Bible.

BETTY BROWN-JOHNSON

ANN BROWN earned her Master's Degree at Texas Tech University in 1963 with a major in English and a minor in psychology. She taught English in 1964 at West Texas State University, while working toward a counseling certificate. When she finished her counseling training, she became the first full-time counselor at WTSU. She also taught one psychology class, and maintained a limited practice at a local medical clinic.

This prolific writer has written for area newspapers for 40 years. Her column *"Our World"* has appeared in *The Canyon News*, her hometown newspaper for the last 20 years. She left WTSU in 1970 to devote more time to writing. She is loved and respected for her neighborhood ministry of "walkiing the walk" as well as "talking the tlak" of the good samaritan.

Our Lord's criterion still stands: "By their fruits ye shall know them." What more need be said to recommend these pages to those who are looking for guidance on these timely subjects of life.

Jimmy Morgan

INTRODUCTION

When I began teaching the Brides' Sunday School Class in our college church about thirty years ago, I was besieged with pleas for help with tottering marriages. Totally lacking in formal training as a counselor, I combed the Scriptures for advice. I tried to find every passage relevant to marriage and the home, and passed them on to the young women in my class.

I also read every book and article I could find on marriage counseling. One article in particular, "Beware the Mind Meddler," convinced me I should go back to school. A Bachelor of Arts in psychology only inspired me to further study. By the time I earned my Master's Degree and finished my training as a professional counselor, I discovered I had been using the best textbook ever written on psychology and counseling all the time: The Bible.

After five years as a counselor at West Texas State University, I resigned to devote full time to writing and Bible teaching.

A local medical doctor said he had observed that healthy people were usually happy ones, and insisted I help him with several of his patients. So I still maintain a limited private practice.

In this book I tried to combine the best psychology I learned, with God's Word to form a simple guide to successful living. I endeavored to list the major choices, decisions, and problems we encounter in life, and point out the promises of God relative to our needs.

CONTENTS

Chapter 1

DO YOU NEED A MIRACLE?

Christians preach, teach, and sing that God is love; God is all-powerful, and He performs miracles. If God created the universe and everything in it, and if it is still His world, why is there so much degradation, grief, and misery everywhere? Why does He not remove all our burdens and heartaches?

Do we follow His directions?

Have you ever experienced a miraculous solution to a problem? Wouldn't you like a few more? When contemplating a life-changing decision, do you feel the need of divine guidance? When you drive across Texas, do you follow a Utah road map? If you want God's guidance, you have to follow His directions.

Do you want a miracle? God wants obedience, and that takes faith. Faith is no great mysterious something to be fervently sought; it is simply believing God will do exactly what He says He will do. An old country preacher used to say, "Faith is believing what you know ain't so." That's not faith; it's foolishness.

But how can you believe God will do what He says He will do unless you know what He says? And when you read God's promises, you will see that every one is conditional. It is useless to expect to claim those promises unless you meet the conditions.

God specifically states He will not do what we want Him to do for us unless we do what He wants us to do for Him (Zech. 7:13). Whether we want a miracle or just God's daily provision, guidance, and protection, we cannot expect His protection unless we obey Him.

How do good parents feel about impudent, disobedient, rebellious children? They probably provide the necessities, but how likely are they to shower such children with extras? God sends the rain on the just and the unjust, but if you expect a miracle, you must love and obey God.

When Joshua and some two million Israelites reached the swollen Jordan River, it was impossible to cross over into the Promised Land. But God never leads His people where His grace cannot sustain them, and He led them to the Jordan.

God's people had to have a miracle to claim the land He promised them. God always keeps His promises-when we obey Him. Joshua said, "Sanctify yourselves" today (get right with God), and tomorrow the Lord will give you the miracle you need (Jos. 3:5).

Joshua told the people to get ready to follow the priests who were carrying the Ark of the Covenant, the symbol of God's presence. It was not until the priests' feet touched the swollen, raging river that the waters parted and opened the way for God's people to cross over on dry land. If the people had not obeyed God, and the leaders had not stepped into the river, there would have been no miracle.

Where are you facing difficulties only a miracle can resolve? And what does God say about your problems?

Remember the leaders were commanded to step into the torrent first, but the others were standing by with their tents folded, and belongings packed, ready to follow wherever God led. We are all leaders in some areas, and followers in others.

What instructions has God given you to execute before you can expect the miracle you need? Remember, God never made a promise without a condition attached to it. We cannot expect God to help us until we meet His conditions.

The word "help" implies mutual effort. If you put forth no effort, do not anticipate God's help. An injured person pinned in the wreckage of an isolated airplane or motor vehicle may be able to do no more than cry out to God. But before you ask Him to do anything, be sure you cannot do it yourself. God will not wash your dishes nor mow your lawn, but He will supply the grace and strength to do it–if you ask. God will always raise up someone to help you do essential tasks you are literally unable to perform. Be sure to be honest with Him. It is so easy to deceive ourselves, we often forget it is impossible to deceive God. He knows so much more about us than we know about ourselves. Do yourself a favor: Ask God what you need to make you happy--then ask Him to help you get it. You could be surprised at what you get.

Few of us have the gift of prophecy; we do not know what the future holds. We do, however, have God's promise that--if we keep His Commandments and trust His guidance, He will direct our paths (Prov. 3:1-6). We need divine guidance and direction as much as we need God's protection, but are we as careful to ask for it? Don't expect His protection while you travel a selfish or wicked path.

We need God's guidance always--even in the little things, but especially when contemplating life-changing decisions. How many mistakes have you already made in that area? You cannot turn back the page, so be sure God is leading before you decide which way to go.

The most important decision ever made concerns our eternal destiny. Of course, no one has to make a decision at all. We can simply drift through time, and slide into eternal darkness when life is over (Rev. 20:11-15). Death is one appointment you can be sure we all will keep. The crowd in hell should be enough to make all rational people avoid it. And you *can* avoid it, but that takes a miracle. And that miracle demands obedience to a very specific command. Are you interested?

Chapter 2

SALVATION

The Lost person's first question may be, "Why do I need salvation? What do I need to be saved from?"

Everyone needs to be saved from being lost. In earlier times, young people said they were going out to seek their fortunes; now they admit they are going out to find themselves. Everyone not in fellowship with his Creator is lost. Can a lost person find himself?

A sense of belonging is essential to emotional health. God sets us in families (Psa. 68:6). We require a sense of identity, and a feeling of personal worth. But first, we need to feel we belong to God. After all, He is the only one who is always available.

When we are born into God's family, we become "A Child of the King"-we belong to Him. This gives us a sense of identity and a definite feeling of personal worth. If God thought we were valuable enough to sacrifice His only Son for our redemption, we must not be as worthless as we sometimes feel.

Of course, when we fail in our responsibilities and sin against God (it is impossible to do one without the other), we feel guilty. And guilt is a miserable, destructive emotion.

God said, "All have sinned and come short of the glory of God" (Rom. 3:23). But read on.

He also said, "The wages of sin is death, but the gift of God is eternal life through Jesus Christ our Lord" (Rom. 6:23).

Babies are born safe in God's care (II Sam. 12:23). Little children are forgiven for His name's sake (I John 2:12). But all who know right from wrong, and fail to do right will be held accountable (James 4:17).

How much sin does it take to separate us from God? Just one (James 2:10). Impossible? If you are suspended from a perilous cliff by a strong chain, and only one link breaks, what happens? But who can live without ever committing one sin? No one.

So that leaves every soul in the clutches of Satan, and in need of a ransom. And even a ransom is not sufficient; the kidnap victim must be willing and able to return to the Father after the ransom has been paid. (Remember Patricia Hearst and the Lindbergh baby? The ransoms were paid but no victims returned.)

But our Creator loves us, and does not want anyone to die (II Peter 3:9; John 3:16). Without faith, however, it is impossible to please God. And we do not have faith unless we believe He exists; He hears us when we call out to Him, has paid the ransom, and that He will keep His promises (Heb. 11:6).

Obviously, it is hopeless to try to claim God's promises until we know what they are, and meet His conditions. God said, 'Whosoever shall call upon the name of the Lord shall be saved" (Joel 2:32; Acts 2:21; Rom. 10:13). "Seek and you shall find" (Matt. 7:7). The lost man knows where he is; it's home he seeks.

What is there to be saved from? The penalty of sin which is death (Rom. 6:23). And that takes a miracle. Jesus compared it to being born all over again (John 3:3). How can any adult manage to be born again? He can't. What did we have to do with our first birth? Nothing-except be there. Our parents, the doctor and nurses took care of the whole affair. But God gave us life in the flesh, and only He can give us spiritual life. Christians can guide, explain, and encourage, but everyone must ask for salvation (the new birth) for himself. Not one person can do it for another.

Before one can ask for anything, however, he has to believe it exists, has to want it, and must know whom to ask, and where. It cost God His only Son to provide our salvation (John 3:16). But He offers it to us as a free gift (Eph. 2:8).

Does that sound too easy? What's to prevent us from accepting God's gift of eternal life, then doing exactly as we please? Surely, God would not give us a gift, then take it back for any reason. There are nasty names for people who do that. We also have God's promises-many of them-that He will not take away His gift. It would not be *eternal* life if it were not guaranteed forever (I John 5:13; 3:14; John 3:16, 4:14; 5:24; 6:47; Heb. 7:25; I Peter 1:3-5, 23, Eph. 1:3-13; 4:30; I Cor. 3:10-15; John 10:27-29).

But what about the people who profess to be Christians-even get religion in a big way, then go out and live as wickedly as the devil could desire.

The Bible explains that, too: When one merely makes a moral reformation, or an empty profession, it cannot last (Luke 11:23-26; II Peter 2:20-22; I John 2:19). But when he is born into the Kingdom of God, he becomes a new creature with a new nature. A washed-up hog is still a hog. But when a swine turns into a lamb, he no longer enjoys a mudhole (II Cor. 5:17). When he is born again, the sinner belongs to a new family, with new and different tastes.

What prevents children doing as they please after birth to earthly parents? Why should it be different with God's family?

There are, however, a few small differences: It is possible to hide things from earthly parents, and eventually one outgrows parental discipline. Nothing can be hidden from God (Ecc. 12:13-14), and we never grow beyond His discipline (Gal. 6:7; Mal. 3:16-18: I Cor. 3:10-15).

Earthly parents love their children no matter what they do (if they are good parents–and God is good). But because they love, they discipline. Can we expect less from God?

Children always resemble their parents–some more, some less. White parents have white children, and black parents have black ones. God's children also resemble Him; again–some more, some less, but the miracle that makes one a child of God makes him want to be like his Father (II Cor. 5:17; Eph. 1:5-13; 4:30-32; John 10:27).

In addition to eternal life with God in glory, salvation gives us joy, love, peace and sustaining grace in this life as well (II Tim. 1:7; I Cor. 10-13). Our earthly blessings are the interest we get on our inheritance laid up for us in heaven (Eph. 1:14).

If there were no heaven to gain nor hell to avoid, it pays to serve Jesus. The fellowship with our Creator in this world is priceless. But to fellowship with God requires obedience. Only one thing can deprive us of that fellowship. Babies are born safe in God's care, but at the age of accountability, we must choose to remain safe in the Father's house, or we can choose to go away (Luke 15:11-13).

Nothing can change the relationship, and only one thing deprives the children of God of fellowship with their Father: disobedience. Doesn't disobedience ruin the fellowship between earthly parents and their children? But loss of fellowship does not sever relationship.

Broken fellowship among relatives is a primary source of depression–the front door to mental illness. Divorce is reported to be more painful than death by people who have suffered both. One out of every ten Americans spends time in a mental hospital. One out of four would profit from it. And if every suicide attempt succeeded, suicide would lead the list as cause of death in America.

Yet God promises perfect peace to all who obey Him. "Thou wilt keep him in perfect peace, whose mind is stayed on Thee: because he trusteth in Thee." (Isa. 26:3; John 6:28-29). Perhaps the major reason so many people reject Christ is because the lives of Christians show no evidence that being a Christian makes them happy.

And how many happy Christians tell all the non-Christians they know that Jesus is the source of their happiness? Do we tell them there is no life in the next world without Christ? (John 14:6), and little hope for happiness in this life as long as they reject Him?

Paul's favorite sermon was telling when and how the Lord saved him. Every Christian can do that. Can you? If not, how do you know you are saved? If you have never asked God to save you, it's quite certain He has not. But if you have not asked Him-ask Him now; He will never refuse a penitent sinner (Rom. 10:13).

After making certain of the destiny of our souls, the next most important commitment we need to make is to a purpose in life. God made us; surely He has something for us to do. To be happy, one must have a purpose for living. What is yours?

Chapter 3

PURPOSE IN LIFE

A popular expression of the NOW generation is, "I have to get out and find myself."

What does it mean to be lost in the physical sense? It means we do not know where we are in relation to home, our destination, or a familiar landmark. It is a helpless feeling, and we do not hesitate to ask for help-if we can find someone to ask.

Can a lost person find himself?

It is not himself he is looking for. He knows where he is, but his surroundings are strange, and he is looking for something familiar. He does not need anyone to tell him where he is; he needs them to guide him to a familiar landmark.

Not one of us knows what the future holds. Next year, next month, tomorrow, or even the next minute is entirely beyond our knowledge or control. As limited as we are, how can we possibly plan ahead for a lifetime?

It's easy-when we walk by faith and not by sight.

We do not know what the future holds. But when we know Him who holds the future, instead of creating problems, our lack of ability to know what lies ahead of us merely adds excitement and zest to life.

It is no more essential for God's children to know the future than it is for an infant to know where his food and dry clothes are coming from. God says we are to depend on Him for our needs and He will supply more than we even think to ask (Eph. 3:20-21; I Peter 5:6-7; Matt. 6:25-34).

No one need wander in the dark seeking God's purpose for life: all we need to do is ask for guidance (Prov. 3:1-6). Nor can we hide from God to withhold our service from Him (Psa. 139:1-15; John 34:21; Ecc. 12:13-14; Matt. 25:14-30).

God never requires anything of us He has not given us the ability to do. He does not ask everyone to sing; a few of us have voices like crows. He only asks us to make a joyful noise (Psa. 95:1-2).

God does not require everyone to preach like Billy Graham, nor sing like Beverly Shea. In fact, the only thing He does require of us is to be faithful (I Cor. 14:1-2), do justly, love mercy, and walk humbly with Him (Micah 6:8). And any Christian can do that.

All men are not given the same talents for the same reason God did not make our bodies all eyes or right arms. Our little toes are as essential to perfect balance as our eyes are to seeing. No member of the human race should be despised any more than any member of our bodies should be considered unnecessary. But if a member of our bodies becomes malignant and threatens to destroy us, we have no choice but eliminate it, however traumatic that may be.

Many of God's children are destined to occupy humble positions in this world. Should we not be as willing to serve wherever God wants us, as we are to expect our children to wash dishes, rake leaves, and take out the garbage? The big trouble with our society is that we all want sewers, but no one wants to dig ditches.

Remember, the Master was as pleased with the service of the man with two talents as He was with the one with five talents (Matt. 25:19-23). The Lord was displeased with the servant He gave only one talent because he failed to use that talent—not because he was limited in ability.

All God asks is that we develop our talents to the utmost, so we can use all the abilities He gives us. God never put a premium on ignorance. All the great leaders in the Bible were well-educated men: Moses, Samuel, and Paul were among the most learned men of their times. God did much maneuvering to place Moses and Samuel in situations where they could get the best training available.

It is true Jesus called several ignorant and unlearned men to follow Him. It is also true He spent three years tutoring them. Could anyone be ignorant after spending three years at the feet of the Master Teacher?

Our timetable does not always operate on God's schedule, however; and sometimes we get impatient to know what His plans are for us. Moses was so sure he was destined to lead his people back to the Promise Land, he could not wait for God to say, "go." But God knew Moses was not ready to go: He thought he could deliver Israel all by himself. When he *was* ready, he didn't believe he could do it *with God's help.* It took forty years in a sheep camp to rid him of the arrogance he acquired in Pharaoh's palace.

The choice to go or stay is not ours. We need to prepare ourselves for whatever task God has for us, and develop all our talents so we will be ready to go whenever and wherever He calls.

Dr. Ben H. Welmaker was pastor of a large Texas church. His people sent him on an evangelistic tour of Europe. He came home aflame with missionary zeal.

The first Sunday morning after Dr. Welmaker returned, he essayed to recruit volunteers for foreign missions, his eyes glowed with exhilaration of his purpose.

"We need *you,* " he exhorted passionately, his words resounded in the packed church. "Those of you who have a college education and seminary training, you owe it to your Maker and your fellowman to give up this easy life. . .devote your energies to taking the Good News to the lost multitudes across the ocean."

The preacher paused, his eyes swept the familiar faces of his congregation, and he automatically cataloged the ones who fulfilled the requirements. One. . .two. . .So few! Disconcerted, he drew his thoughts back to his message.

"In this Country we hear the gospel on radio, see it proclaimed on television, and we sit in our luxurious churches, listening to sermon after sermon. We are gospel soaked, while people in foreign nations are starving for the Word of God."

At the invitation, several came forward to volunteer, but not one who was prepared. In their response to their pastor's enthusiasm, they forgot the years of college and seminary training required.

Graciously, Dr. Welmaker thanked the volunteers for their willingness to sacrifice their personal desires for others. "I'm sorry, he said again and again. "This work demands years of training. We love and appreciate you for offering. As soon as you are prepared. . ." Suddenly, in a blinding moment of revelation, the Lord spoke to the pastor: "You are already prepared: why don't you go?"

Dr. Welmaker resigned his church immediately. With his wife and three children, he offered his services to the Foreign Mission Board. They did not send them to Europe, however, as he anticipated, but to South America. To his utter amazement he found himself President of a fifteen-acre pasture in Cali, Colombia.

Through years of patient toil, Dr. Welmaker and his family watched that empty pasture develop into a seminary that has sent hundreds of young people out to serve God in South America.

That preacher never dreamed God wanted

him in Colombia, but when the call came, he was prepared to go.

We are only responsible for the talents God gives us; if we develop them to the best of our ability, and are willing to follow where He leads, there is no doubt we can find His purpose for our lives. If you want a call like Dr. Welmaker had, live close enough to the Lord to hear His voice when He speaks. We already have His promise to direct us if we ask (Prov. 3:5-6; Matt. 7:7-11).

Never think God's children are expected to fight their way through this confusing world alone. If our Creator was careful to perfume a rose, ruffle a petunia, and monitor a sparrow's fall, don't you believe He is concerned about His crowning creation? But there is not much coasting on the road to a happy, successful life, because success is not found in that direction.

Skeptics ask, "Does the universe have direction? Does life have purpose?"

Does day follow night?

Life's preparation takes money as well as time and energy. Do you already need a miracle to solve your financial difficulties?

The only call God gives us is to follow Him (John 10:27; II Tim. 1:9). If our vocation is to be a Christian, it matters little what we do to earn a living–but it matters tremendously that we earn it. We lose the respect of the world we hope to win if we do not earn an honest living. Working at a respectable task is mandatory for

God's children—no peddling alcohol or any other destructive substance.

Keeping our finances in good order is essential to our Christian witness. Would you like to know the best way to do it?

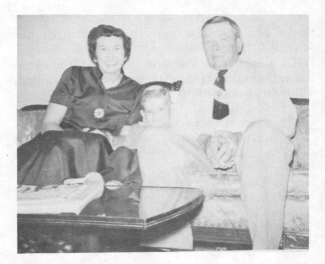

Home Sweet Home

Chapter 4

FINANCIAL DIFFICULTIES

Prior to any discussion of finances, remember the real measure of wealth is how much you would be worth if you lost all your money. Success is not wealth but happiness.

It is most difficult, however, to be concerned about a purpose in life, spiritual things, your loved ones, or the state of your church, community, or the universe, while your stomach gnaws with hunger, or you are too exhausted to think. Check carefully to see what obedience God demands before He can send the miracle you need to solve your money problems.

Wealth, of course, is relative. True wealth is the possession of whatever brings happiness, contentment, and a sense of personal worth. Anyone who lacks self-esteem is poor-regardless of his bank balance.

If everyone suddenly received a million dollars, this world would be in big trouble. Few rich farmers would plow or plant. Would rich bakers and canners bake or can? Rich shopkeepers would close their shops and go see the world. Millionaire sheepmen would not shear smelly sheep. No millionaire would dig sewers, mine coal, weave cloth, or repair leaky pipes. With a million dollars each, we'd all stay cold and hungry-until we learned money is useless where no goods and services are available.

The first thing you need to do is to evaluate the source of your financial troubles. What is your sense of values? Are you in too big a hurry to get rich? (Prov. 28:22) Are you stingy? (Prov. 11:24; II Cor. 9:6; Mal. 3:10-11) Are you stubborn? (Prov. 13:18) Are you lazy? (Prov. 6:6-11; 12:24; II Thess. 2:10) Do you smoke, drink, or spend too much money on recreation or food? (Prov. 23:21) Are you a poor manager? (Prov. 28:19-20) If you are unable to judge yourself on these questions, ask an older brother or your best friend; either will be delighted to tell you. (Don't expect God to solve your financial problems while you burn up, drink up, or fritter away the money He has already given you.)

If you find yourself "not guilty" on all the above, perhaps God wants you to make a major change in your vocation, location, living standard, or some of the procedures you use in earning or managing your money.

What is your material goal? Wealth? Fun? Security? The only real financial security or enjoyment is freedom from debt (Prov. 22:7). Many scriptures warn against borrowing. It is seldom wise to borrow for anything that decreases in value. And a home and land are about the only things, properly cared for, that *increase* in value.

Borrowing violates scripture (Rom. 13:8); produces bondage (Prov. 22:7), and presumes upon the future (James 4:13-14). It also tends to limit God from withholding harmful things from you (Isa. 55:8-9).

The majority of us get into financial trouble the same way the farmer did who raised a huge crop of sweet potatoes. When he began to dig his potatoes, he could find no market for them, so he piled them on the ground. After about three days they began to rot. The farmer cried out, "Oh, Lord, what am I going to do with these sweet potatoes?"

The Lord said, "What sweet potatoes?"

We should ask the Lord about an investment *before* we make it instead of waiting until we get in trouble with it.

Financial freedom has three sides. Be sure you are obedient to God on all three before you ask for help. The first side is giving; the second is receiving, and the third is spending. The best way to get into trouble is to reverse that order—and many people do that very thing.

God said the first tenth of all our increase belongs to Him (Ex. 23:19a; Lev. 27: 30-32; Prov. 3:9-10; Luke 6:38; Mal. 3:10). And if we don't give it to God, Satan collects it (Mal. 3:11).

But don't the wicked prosper? Oh, yes. Sometimes Satan collects from us in this world, sometimes in the next. He will have no chance to collect from God's children in the next world, so He has to get his dues here.

We receive our money by God's grace, diligent labor, and creative resourcefulness (Prov. 6:6-8; 10:4-5; 31:10-27) We should spend it wisely (Prov. 3:5-6; 21.27; II Kings 4:7; Rom. 3:8).

Jesus said that our heavenly Father knows we need food, clothing, and shelter; and He has an abundant supply of those necessities to give us. Before He showers on us the blessings He has prepared for us, however, we must devote our time and energies to promoting His Kingdom (Matt. 6:24-33).

Chasing wealth is much like a dog chasing his tail. If he catches it, what has he accomplished? But if he goes on about his affairs, his tail will follow him, and perform its proper function.

Jesus said the greatest commandment was to love God supremely, and your neighbor as yourself (Mark 12:29-31). Love for God and our neighbors is not expressed through receiving; love is giving. "God so loved the world that he gave. . ." (John 3:16)

God said, "If you love me, keep my commandments" (John 24:15). His first commandment is, "You shall have no other gods before me" (Ex. 20:3).

Perhaps you're saying, "That's good. I don't worship other gods. I never bowed down to an idol, and I have no intention of doing so."

Are you sure?

How do we idolize a person, place, or thing? We love. And we show our love by devoting time, energy, and money to the object of our affections.

No one is completely objective about himself. It would be difficult to honestly say what has first place in our hearts. But we can be objective about the way we spend our time, energy, and money.

Our Creator is most generous. He did not ask for the lion's share of the wealth He has given us–only one tenth. He did not ask for the major portion of our time–only one day in seven. He did, however, ask for first place in our hearts, and that can be manifested only through love and obedience–which are two sides of the same coin.

If that is true, can you honestly say God has first place in your life? Do you dedicate one day in seven to Him? Do you reverence His Day? His name? His house? His people?

Do you honor your parents, and show kindness and courtesy to your neighbors: God did not say honor your parents provided they are honorable; He just said honor them. And He did not say love your neighbor provided he loves you. He said love him as you love yourself.

The man who loves his neighbor will not kill him or commit adultery with his wife, daughter, or sister. We do not steal from the people we love, lie about them, or covet their possessions. These are destructive acts; would you destroy yourself? You do not have to approve of your neighbor to love him.

There is a vast difference between loving people and liking them. We love people in spite of their faults; we like them because of charming qualities they possess. Most of us have more faults than charm, so we don't always like ourselves very well.

Has anyone ever failed you, disappointed you, or abused you as many times as you have let yourself down? Yet don't you go right on loving and forgiving yourself, and providing your necessities of life? Do you want to do yourself harm?

Actually, you must love yourself before you can love your neighbor. People who hate themselves usually make very poor neighbors. Think of the people you know who hate themselves; don't you prefer to avoid them? Is there anything more depressing than to hear one apologize for his very existence, and recount all his inadequacies? He is even more disgusting than his counterpart who brags and boasts continually in a vain effort to hide his deficiencies.

To love your neighbor does not mean you have to approve of everything he does and says, or that you want to be his bosom companion. It simply means you do him no harm, and that you will do him good if the need and opportunity arises.

God said we had to love our neighbors; He did not say we had to like them.

If you love your neighbor, you do not want to defraud him in any way. This means you give an honest day's wages for a day's work, and you give an honest day's work for a day's wages. You pay your debts. Not to do so is to steal from your neighbors. For any person to live on welfare who is able to work is also stealing (II Thess. 7:12).

What really has first claim on your time, energy, and money? Is it your children? House?

Automobile? Hobby? Television set? Boat? Summer cabin? Football games? Bowling ball? Food? Clothes? Or is it recreation?

Does the Lord's day find you in His house? Or are you at work, asleep, at the lake, or at a ball game?

Many professing Christians insist they have to work on Sunday, or it's the only day they have to sleep, or visit, or catch up on the week's chores. But God placed more emphasis on keeping His day holy than He did all the other commandments combined. And He sent His chosen people into seventy years of cruel captivity because they profaned His holy day (II Chron. 36:21; Neh. 13:18). Will He be more lenient with twentieth century Christians?

Do you give God His tithe? He said the tithe "is the Lord's" (Lev. 27:30-32). He did not say it ought to be, but "it is." That means if we do not give it to Him, we have stolen it. And He did not confine the statement to Christians but applied it to all men.

If you want God to bless you financially, you must obey Him (Mal. 3:6-11). And remember the leaders go first. The head of the house should step out on faith. He should lead his family in worship, tithing, Bible study, and Christian ministry.

Does your family spend as much time in worship, Bible study, and visiting or ministering in His name as you do watching television, attending ball games, or boating?

After thinking that question over, are you sure you have no idols, and that God has first place in your life?

You want a financial miracle? God wants obedience. Obey Him and you have His promise to take care of your financial problems (Prov. 3:9-10).

David said, "I have been young, and now am old; yet have I not seen the righteous forsaken, nor his seed begging bread" (Psa. 37:25). God did not promise to make us rich (riches are seldom a blessing), but He did promise to give us more than we are able to receive (Mal. 3:10). Your ability to receive usually depends on your dedication to God.

The only people who think houses, lands, bank accounts, luxury automobiles, fashionable clothes, fame, and social position bring happiness are the ones who have never attained those things.

How dedicated are you? Are you willing to make the promotion of the kingdom of God the most important thing in your life? If so, get busy, and you are ready to claim God's promise to clear up your financial difficulties (Matt. 6;33), and lead you to find purpose in life–and joy. To find joy, you must have someone with whom you can share your life (Gen. 2:18). The first thing God ever said was *not good* was for man to live alone. Do you have a partner? If not, are you looking for one? Do you know God's guidelines?

Chapter 5

CHOOSING A MATE

The French say marriage is either a duet or a duel.

Your choice of a mate is one of life's three most important choices. If you are not in the right relationship with God, however, and have not found His purpose for your life, you are not really qualified to choose a mate at all. Ungodly people who lead purposeless lives seldom find mates who please them-though they may marry many times.

Henry Ford said his formula for a happy marriage was the same one he used to make a successful car: "Stick to one model."

If all divorced persons were forced to be reconciled to their mates-or live alone, divorce statistics would plummet.

Battered wives and neglected husbands usually defend their remaining with cruel mates by saying even brutality is peferable to loneliness.

It is *not good* for one to live alone (Gen. 2:18), nor is abuse easy to take or unavoidable: Any two people who will get right with God, can get right with each other.

Suppose, however, your spouse refuses to get right with God, or has a bad personality problem?

There is no problem God cannot cure, but

BOTH parties do have to be willing to turn it over to Him (Mark 10:27).

Of course, if you failed to consult God in the choice of your mate, your situation may be like the farmer's sweet potatoes.

It is impossible to be sufficiently committed to a *person* to keep a marriage together; one must be committed to marriage.

But what about the one who had no choice in the matter? If your husband takes off with his secretary, or if your wife elopes with your "best friend", is the abandoned mate doomed to live alone?

There is no question that God wants His children to be happy. (John 10:7-11; Psalm 1:1-3). Psalm 84:11 is a concise picture of God's love for mankind: "For the Lord God is a sun and shield: the Lord will give grace and glory: no good thing will he withhold from them that walk uprightly."

We know the sun sustains life. A shield protected a soldier's vitals in battle. Everyone has to have a little grace and glory to survive. And He promises good things to His children who do right (obey God).

All any rational person wants is to be happy. Look around you. As a rule, are the divorced people who remarry happier than the ones who remain single? Or did they climb back into the same kind of boat?

One man eloped with his secretary, leaving five children, and his wife of 20 years, to fend for themselves. A year later, however, he called his wife, and made abject apology. He said if she could not find it in her heart to take him back, he would kill himself.

The children were so hurt, they said, "Let him go!" But the wife sweetly forgave him and let him come home. And the children are glad-now.

They have celebrated their 65th wedding anniversary, surrounded by children, grand-children, and great-grandchildren. Friends and relatives admired their courage: His in admitting his mistake, doing his best to correct it, and returning to face family and friends. Her's for her forgiving spirit, and for being big enough to swallow her pride for the good of all concerned.

Pride makes a bad bedfellow, never puts food on the table, and provides a poor parent for orphan children.

A woman who professes to be a Christian (She is a church member.) has been married 5 times. Every husband except the first one sent her to the hospital with broken bones. She is currently single, and wishes she had remained so.

God's children who live in obedience to Him are always happier than the ones who do not. Don't children who obey earthly parents fare better? And remember, just as you do not spank your neighbor's child, God confines His disipline to His own.

If you can do wrong and get by with it, you can be sure you are not God's child. "As many as I love, I rebuke and chasten: be zealous, therefore, and repent (Rev. 3:19).

If you are God's child, and living in disobedience to Him, Don't expect to be happy.

A man who became a Christian at age 47, said, "I got along fine until I trusted Christ as my Savior; I have been in hot water ever since."

He was under the delusion that God's children should be happy-always. After ten years of trying to cope with one disaster after another, he said he finally realized "God does not spank the devil's children."

Now he is grateful God loves him enough to rebuke him when he does wrong, and he realizes he must "clean up his act," and accept Christ as his Lord as well as his Savior.

People usually say relative to one who has passed the prime age for marrying, "Oh, well, when the right one comes along. . ."

Why would anyone in his right mind leave such a life-changing choice to chance? When you decide to buy a new wardrobe, an automobile, or a house, do you depend on taking whatever you happen to run across?

Hardly! You shop long and carefully. If people would be half as careful about the mates they choose, divorce would go out of style.

Oh, but "love is blind," and "you never get to know one until you marry anyway." There is enough truth in both statements to convince almost anyone that selecting the right life companion requires a miracle. Of course, *being* the right companion is most important–and that needs even a greater miracle. What are God's rules to be obeyed before one can expect those miracles?

First of all, Matthew 6:33. Then earnestly seek God's will in the matter, ask Him to lead you to the right companion, and claim His promises in John 15:7 and Matthew 7:7. Be sure you meet His condition of not marrying an unbeliever (II Cor. 6:14), a near kinsman (Lev. 18:6), a divorced person (Mark 10:11-12; Rom. 7:2-3), or one not of your own race (Ezra 10:2).

The example given in the Bible for a God-approved marriage is to marry one from your own race, religious faith, and social station (Gen. 27:46-28:1-2; 24:1-4). If you ignore God's admonitions in selecting a mate, don't blame Him if you get one you can't live with.

Marriage is a working arrangement, however, and even marriages "made in heaven" require maintenance work by both partners. God surely chose Rebekah for Isaac, and she met all the requirements, but they had far from an ideal marriage (Gen. 24:38-48; 25:28; 27:5-17). Jacob did not want Leah, and never loved her, yet God blessed him through his faithful Leah far more than through his beloved Rachel.

The Bible is an objective account of the people of God and His dealings with them. Just because an event is recorded in the Scripture does not mean God approved it. Abraham had two wives, but not with God's approval. And the children of those wives are still hating and killing each other to this very hour.

Marriage is a God-ordained institution. If you want yours to be successful, try reading the directions before you start putting it together. Marriage with peace is Paradise, without it–it's Purgatory.

But with all the problems marriage brings, is it worth the effort?

Do you want paradise? Then take the risk. But be sure you build it according to the Master Builder's blueprint.

A home that is well constructed is like a well-built house–it gives you few problems.

The most important facet in marriage is not that a couple like the same books or entertainment. It's whether basically they are the same kind of people. If you have the same attitude toward things, the same goals, background, heredity, and traditions you will be comfortable together. And comfort is the essential marital cement.

Marriage is somewhat like a television set. When you stop to think how complicated it is and how many things could go wrong with it, the fact that it runs at all is a miracle. But just as a TV set that's basically sound can generally be made to run with a bit of expert tinkering, so most marriages in which the partners are comparatively adult, well-adjusted people, can be made to function to the mutual satisfaction of both parties by a bit of common sense and patience.

Even if you aren't long on patience, the next

chapter offers some suggestions for staying out of the divorce court.

Two Equals One

Chapter 6

MARITAL PROBLEMS

Marriage is often compared to a hot bath: after you have been in it for a while, it's not so hot. True. But it can always be warmed up; the hot water faucet is marked, "Mutual Concern."

According to government statistics and many private polls, about one third of all American marriages end in divorce (one half of the teens), and eighty percent of the couples who stay together are unhappy. So if you have no marital problems, you are an exception. But don't skip this chapter! If you don't need help, you have friends and relatives who do.

Marital discord destroys a vital emotion: a sense of belonging. If you cannot feel your mate is loyal to you, whom can you trust? The two of you are supposed to be one flesh; you belong to each other. That sense of belonging (a necessity to emotional health) is the cement that holds marriages together.

Almost all marital problems originate in disobedience to the first commandment God gave to young marrieds in Genesis 2:24. "Leave" and "cleave." The leaving will eliminate a host of marital discord, and the cleaving will will likely take care of the rest.

High on the list of requirements for cleaving is loyalty. All of us have our idiosyncrasies. To us they seem natural and normal. To others they are strange. As you discovered your mate's amazing little quirks, did you discuss them with your friends and relatives, or were you loyal enough to him to keep them to yourself?

Love and loyalty are like two sides of the same coin. Disloyalty will destroy love. Mates should be loyal to each other in obedience to God-and as a matter of honor and principle. You make no one think any more of you or less of your mate by discussing his private affairs with them, but it can wreck your home. And your sex life is high on the list of private affairs.

The home was the first institution God created. All others grow out of it. No church or any other institution is any better than the homes that make up its membership.

When God created the home, He ordained that the man should be the head of it. The only creatures ever born with two heads are freaks, and they don't survive. No home can survive with two heads-nor can it survive with none.

The home is a precious gift; it is the one institution everyone must belong to if he is to be happy. Without a home, man finds very little to live for. Nothing else can compensate. And it takes at least two people to make a home.

The first thing God ever said was not good was for man to live alone (Gen. 2:18), so God made woman to be his helper-not his manager. Being a husband is like any other job: It's much easier if you're the boss.

Many highly successful and wealthy career women are frustrated and unhappy. They would gladly exchange their lucrative positions for humble houses with husbands and children.

Because the home is God's greatest gift to mankind, the role of homemaker is an honorable and coveted one. Why, then, are there so many frustrated, nervous, miserable wives who prefer any kind of work outside the home to their role as homemaker?

The situation is a complex one that defies a simple answer, but the root of the problem is disobedience to God; perhaps not so much the couple involved as their parents and their parents before them. Our Creator ordained that the husband be head of the house (Eph. 5:22-24). He also commanded that a husband love and cherish his wife as his own body (Eph. 5:28, 29).

No wife has anything to fear in obeying a husband who loves her. He will never demand anything of her that is not part of her duty or for her own good. And no wife can be happy who does not do her duty. But the average American wife will run over her husband if he will allow it–and despise him if he does.

A woman instinctively wants her husband to be head of the house. She will not respect him if he's not. But respect cannot be commanded; it must be earned.

Probably the most important factor causing the breakdown of the American home is the lack of a good example; there is no substitute for it. The best of rules and inhibitors are useless if not backed up by a decent example. Children from one-parent homes have no opportunity to observe how husbands and wives should treat each other. But whatever "sins of the fathers" you may have inherited, your marriage will still be what you make it.

One of the "termites" that few marriages can survive is jealousy. If a triangle actually exists, something constructive should be done about it. If no triangle exists, jealousy may create one.

If a husband doesn't need watching, it's a waste of time to watch him. And if he does need watching, it's a waste of time to watch him.

Where there is no grounds for jealousy, it usually stems from a neurotic fear-or a guilty conscience. But it can be lethal to love, because it is definitely a vote of no confidence in one's mate. And faith and love are inseparable.

Regardless of the problems that arise, mates should communicate their feeling to each other. Couples who *talk out* their troubles seldom walk out on them.

For a man to be head of his house does not mean he should be a dictator, a bully, or a Simon Legree. God commands exactly the opposite: The husband is to love and cherish his wife (Eph. 5:28-33), protect and provide for her (I Tim. 5:8), and lead her in spiritual matters (I Tim 2:12).

If a wife finds her role as homemaker unattractive, perhaps it's because her husband has failed to love her. Loving her requires being her protector, provider, and spiritual leader. And probably he failed because his father failed to set a good example before him. Or the wife may reject his leadership because she had a cruel father or a domineering mother.

There is probably no area in which "the sins of the fathers" are more fatally visited upon the children than in the creation of homes. Ungodly parents can certainly lessen the chances of their children being able to establish satisfactory homes, but somebody needs to break the chain.

Human nature being what it is, no one can expect perfect parents or a perfect companion. When God said "husbands love your wives" He did not say provided they are lovable. And when He said "wives obey your husbands," He did not add provided they are kind, and provident.

The basis of most marital problems is a misunderstanding of the meaning of love. Many unhappy young marrieds wail, "All I want is love." But love is not receiving; love is giving ("God so loved the world that he gave. . . .").

Money and sex are the most common complaints in family rows. The stingy husband is not loving his wife. And the spendthrift wife is neither loving nor obeying her husband.

When a mature couple love each other, both are primarily interested in *giving* satisfaction-not *getting* it.

A hardworking, generous, considerate husband who wants to give his family everything he *can* afford is not likely to have much trouble convincing his wife there are some things they *cannot* afford.

And the wife who wants to make her husband happy will not deprive him of sexual satisfaction (I Cor. 7:2-5), however obnoxious sex may be to her.

Too many people love their mates the same way they "love" oranges: They squeeze all they can get out of them, and then throw them away. You can't love an orange; you can only enjoy it. But if you confine your relationship to your mate to the joy you can get *out* of him, you are not likely to have him around long to enjoy.

The majority of our marital problems can be traced to disobedience to God. In the first place, God said, Be not unequally yoked together with unbelievers (II Cor. 6:14).

There is no scriptural basis, however, for a Christian to dissolve his marriage because he is married to an unbeliever. Marriage is an institution. One should make careful investigation before entering any institution, but having entered it, you are subject to its rules; you cannot expect the rules to be changed to please you. And when you have become "one flesh" with an unbeliever, you can no more be twain than you could with a believer.

Paul did say if you are married to an unbeliever, and he chooses to depart, let him depart (I Cor. 7:12-15). But he did not say dissolve the marriage and marry someone else. It is not divorce, however, that God forbids, but remarriage (I Cor. 7:10-11).

When we open doors to the future, we automatically close them on the past; there is no turning back. A divorce cannot return the girlhood that is gone forever.

If every Christian would be careful to select only a Christian companion, the battle would be half won to begin with. Then if the husband would assume his divine role as a loving provider, protector, and leader, the average wife would probably find her role as wife and mother so fulfilling she would have no desire to leave the sheltering walls of her home.

The average American home has departed so far, however, from the divine pattern, few husbands, wives, or children even know what it is. A generation ago, a wife and mother who worked outside the home (when it was not financially necessary) was viewed with suspicion. Now the reverse is true. Many young men refuse to marry girls who have no salable skill, or who refuse to help them with the finances.

God's plan is for a man to make the living, and his wife to make the living worthwhile (Prov. 31:10-31). If a man fails to provide the living, his wife may lack the time, energy, and incentive to make the living worthwhile. On the other hand, if a wife fails to make the living worthwhile, her husband may get tired making a living for her.

God commands a husband to love his wife, but there is no place in the Bible where a woman is commanded to love her husband; she is only commanded to respect and obey him. There are probably several reasons for this. In the first place, men have the choice, and a man seldom marries a woman unless he loves her and wants to marry her. Women marry men for all sorts of reasons.

In Bible times, of course, women had no choice at all of their husbands. Even "liberated" American women do not have too much choice. Men are still prone to run from women who openly try to marry them. If a woman cannot choose her husband, she can hardly be expected to love him. God never asks the impossible. But if she is not prepared to make him a good wife-and that includes respecting and obeying him-she should not accept him as a husband. She does have that choice.

When God said husband and wife would be one flesh (Eph. 5:31), that means a husband should have the same access to his wife's body that he has to his own. So a woman who denies her husband sexual satisfaction is disobedient to God (I Cor. 7:1-5). And a husband who fails to share his earnings with his wife is equally disobedient (Eph. 5:25).

A husband who allows his wife to spend more than he earns, however, is out of the will of God (Eph. 5:24) as much as the one who refuses to support her (I Tim. 5:8). Actually the finances should be handled by the one who handles them best. A wife who proves she cannot handle money should not resent her husband controlling the bank account. And a man who cannot manage money well should turn that task over to his wife if she can do better.

The majority of young marrieds have some money and sex difficulties. But any two people who will get right with God can get right with each other.

There is no such thing as **one** happy partner in a marriage. Both are happy or both are unhappy. So if you want to be happy, do your best to make your companion happy, and your children. When you try to make your family happy, they will probably try to make you happy, too. And isn't that your ultimate goal in all your relationships–to be happy?

When a man is doing the best he can to provide for his family, his wife should be satisfied. But she does have the right to expect his best. And when a woman makes herself pleasantly available in the sex relationship, her husband should not demand more.

Many marriage counselors insist you should accept your mate exactly the way he is and make no attempt to change him. Granted, it is wiser to spend more time making over him than making him over. But everyone is always in a state of becoming. What your mate becomes largely depends on you, whether you bring out the best in him or the worst.

The only constant we have in this world is change. How can two people become one without changing? The fusion or compromise that is essential if two people are to live together happily requires change.

People who do not try to change their mates usually end up changing mates.

Some disagreement in marriage is a normal part of healthy change. Mates simply need to learn to disagree agreeably. If your mate has habits, mannerisms, or personality traits that drive you up the wall, don't sulk; talk it out with him. Then when he tells you about your habits, etc., that rasp his nerves-listen, and both of you will gradually become nicer people. It is a simple matter of applying the Golden Rule (Matt. 7:13). If you aren't willing to change your annoying ways, don't ask your mate to change his.

No two people can love each other continuously. In fact, they may even hate each other occasionally. If they never contemplate divorce, it's probably because they prefer murder. But, however much you may want to drown your mate today, tomorrow you will probably be glad you didn't. God did not condemn righteous anger; He just said don't stay angry (Eph. 4:26).

A wife may leave her husband through no fault of his, because she may not have wanted to marry him in the first place. But a man usually marries because he loves and wants *that* woman. And unless he is emotionally ill or a congenital psychopath, he is not likely to leave a wife who kisses him goodbye in the morning, meets him with a smile when he returns, and keeps him comfortable.

A comfortably clean house (not so nasty nice he can't enjoy it), good meals served at his convenience, plenty of clean clothes, and pleasant companionship are all essential to a man's comfort. The wife who provides these necessities for her husband need have little fear that he will abandon her.

At least eighty percent of the task of making a home is the wife's responsibility. So eight out of ten homes that break up probably fail because the wife failed in her role as a homemaker. And divorces usually create more problems than they solve. In the second marriage the disgruntled wife is likely to find that she only exchanged one set of faults for worse ones.

It is often said that the perfect wife is one who does not expect a perfect husband. Respectful, obedient, helpful wives usually have loving, faithful, provident husbands. It would be difficult to say, however, which comes first; but Peter did exhort Christian wives to set good examples for ungodly husbands.

A good marriage has been compared to a harbor in a storm. And a bad marriage is more like a storm in a harbor.

The miracle every Christian needs who is married to an unbeliever is the conversion of that lost companion. But before you can expect that miracle, you must be willing to live in obedience to God yourself.

Many lost husbands have said of their wives who profess to be Christians, "Being a Christian has not seemed to help my wife; why should I try it?" This cannot be said of the obedient Christian woman.

If this is your husband's complaint, what are you doing wrong? Are you unpleasant? Men usually will tolerate almost anything from their wives as long as they are loving and pleasant.

The Christian wife who wants to win her husband to the Lord should ask herself first, "Am *I* obedient to God?" To obey God, a woman must obey her husband. And that one command is enough to keep many wives out of the will of God.

Any woman who obeys God is not likely to have any marital problems she can't handle. Because obeying God includes obeying her husband, and obeying her husband includes taking care of his physical comfort, his sexual desires, his finances, and his need for companionship. To be Christian, a wife must be agreeable and industrious.

And the man who obeys God should have very few marital problems. A wife's first desire is usually to be loved. A husband can't obey God without loving, cherishing, and providing for his wife. Just what does a cherished woman have to complain about?

The universal goal–whether conscious or unconscious–is to seek pleasure and avoid pain. If we contribute to the pleasure of our mates (and the same is true of all our associates), they seek our companionship. If we cause them pain, they avoid us as much as possible.

The man who lingers at the corner bar, pool hall, or coffee shop, probably does so because he dreads to go home and face an unpleasant wife. The longer he lingers the more unpleasant she is likely to become. If she is not wise enough to break the vicious circle, the marriage usually breaks.

There is an old maxim that says "A woman will either lift a man up to her level, or drag him down to her level." That may be a bit hard on male pride. But before men discount it, they should remember what Eve did to Adam. Apparently, he had not been tempted by the forbidden fruit until Eve enticed him.

Peter admonished husbands and wives to live together in peace and harmony so their spiritual lives could be fruitful (I Peter 3:1-12). How can people serve God when they spend all their time and energies fighting each other?

The old fairy tale ending, "And so they were married and lived happily ever after" has deceived many young marrieds into thinking marriages just naturally turn out well. Happy homes are no more native products than rose gardens: They both take careful planning, planting, and pruning.

Probably the best advice an officiating minister could give the young couple he marries would be that almost nothing merits harsh words or ill feelings between them. They will disagree on many things, of course, on their journey to the spiritual unity a happy marriage requires. But they need to learn to disagree agreeably.

Investigate the "ideal" marriage, and you usually find a couple who are careful not to provoke each other. Talk to the man who cuts off his wife's charge accounts, and you will likely learn that she opened them without his knowledge or consent. A harmonious marriage requires mutual consideration and cooperation.

The things you quarrel about are not nearly as important or influential on your lives and happiness as the fact that you quarrel. Few men can tolerate disapproval from their wives. And rejecting them sexually is the most intolerable disapproval of all.

Every institution in the world rests on the home. If the foundation is destroyed, what will become of the superstructure?

What man would allow a neighbor to pick up his newspaper every morning, or filch the milk from his door? Yet he will stand meekly by while his wife and children are stolen.

A woman may drive for miles to shop to avoid meeting "her clothes" at social functions, and refuse to share her choicest recipes. But if another woman tries to appropriate her husband, she dashes down to the divorce court and throws him at her.

"I have my pride!" she says.

Pride makes a sorry bedfellow, never pays the

grocery bill, and functions mighty poorly as a father for orphan children.

Before you decide your mate is responsible for all your problems, do a little recollecting. Were you divinely happy before you were married? If you were frustrated and miserable when you were single, there is no magic in a marriage ceremony to automatically fill your life with bliss. Life is what *you* make it–married or single.

Harmony in the home must begin with righteousness in the hearts of the people who live there. And righteousness begins with obedience to God.

The miracle you need to solve your marital problems awaits only your willingness to obey God. "If ye abide in me, and my words abide in you, ye shall ask what ye will, and it shall be done unto you " John 15:7.

A young couple who were sweethearts in junior high school finally made it to the marriage altar after ten long years of waiting. He spent four years in the navy, and came home to finish his schooling on his GI Bill. She was an only child from a broken home. Abandoned by her father, she worked her way through college while supporting her neurotic mother. Life was hard for the young lovers.

Marriage had been their goal for so many years that the honeymoon was actually a let-down. Both bride and groom were virgins; they found it impossible to suddenly turn on feelings they had squelched for so many years.

They were bitterly disappointed at their reactions. The newlyweds secretly wanted to call it quits when they came "home" from their "honeymoon." But their Christian conviction that marriage was sacred checked them. And how would they face family and friends after their beautiful wedding, and all the gifts that had been showered on them?

But after three months of pure misery, the husband offered to transfer to a job in another state so his wife could save face. She could not leave her job, so she could explain the separation as an economic necessity.

The unhappy bride appreciated the generous offer, but she refused to accept it. She said "I was not happy before we married, and I've been plagued with depression all my life. However, with the help of a Christian counselor, I managed to survive. Let's find a good counselor, and with God's help we'll work out our problems."

Every couple needs to solve their adjustment dilemmas before the children come. The fewer marital problems you have, the less likely you are to have rebellious children. But if you already have rebellious children, what do you do with them?

Chapter 7

REBELLIOUS CHILDREN

Children, like a garden, produce both weeds and flowers. If they grow up with an abundance of love and affection, where joy and peace prevail, they blossom with all the virtues they were naturally endowed. If they are denied love and approval, or if they are neglected and abused, and grow up in the midst of strife, inconsistency, and insecurity, all the flowers in them wither and the weeds take over.

If you make your children happy when they are little, you will make them happy twenty years later in retrospect.

As a parent, one's highest ambition should be to water the flowers in their children, and take care never to water the weeds. Those weeds eventually must be reckoned with as they turn your sweet babies into sullen rebels.

Nothing brings parents more grief than rebellious children, and they have been with us always. Remember Adam's petulant Cain who murdered his righteous brother out of pure jealousy? And Isaac's hairy Esau who despised his birthright, and traded it for a bowl of stew? And David's vain Absalom who tried to kill his own doting father, and steal his kingdom? In fact, the pages of history are littered with the rebellious sons of kings who murdered their royal fathers.

And one of the uglier facets of our contemporary society is the appalling number of middleaged Americans who have their elderly parents declared mentally incompetent so they can snatch the old folks' possessions. Is it any wonder children rebel against such cheats?

Then there are the fathers who walk out on their wives and leave them with a house full of children to rear and support. And almost as ugly are the wives who throw their husbands out, then, through alimony and child support, fasten themselves like so many leeches to the poor men, and suck every drop of blood they can get out of them without giving one thing in return.

How can children respect such parents?

It seems that Godly and ungodly parents alike, however, may produce rebellious children. David had them, and so did evil Sennacherib. The Assyrian assassin conquered practically the known world but could not rule his own house. After his humiliating defeat by the God of Israel, he was murdered as he worshipped in the temple of his idol god. Two of his sons carved him up with their swords, while a third took over the kingdom.

What, then, can be done about rebellious children?

There is no guarantee that any child will not rebel. All children seem to be born rebellious. As soon as an infant passes the da-da stage, his first clearly enunciated word is usually a resounding "No!" Apparently, some children are born with more weeds than others (Prov. 17-21).

Children may become rebellious at any age. Certainly, Jacob's ten sons were grown men when they plotted to kill their innocent young brother, Joseph. They decided to sell him into slavery instead, not out of mercy–greed! But Jacob had watered the weeds in the ten by showering all his love and affection on his younger sons.

There are two ages, however, that are especially rebellious. As infants emerge from infancy to childhood (usually around three), and as they pass from childhood to adulthood (generally about fifteen), they are especially obnoxious. The three-year-old is still small enough to be spanked, and therefore endurable. The fifteen-year-old is certainly not young enough to spank, and often not endurable.

If there is no guarantee children will not rebel, what hope is there for parents? The best defense parents have against bringing up rebels is to give them love and approval, and set a good example of conformity before them. Loving Christian parents who do their best to conform to all the laws of God and man seldom rear rebellious children.

Numerous young couples have been so disgusted with the dirty, hairy, rebellious teenagers that they have determined not to take a chance on producing such creatures by having no children at all. Their attitude is certainly understandable. When people get old and help-less, however, it's mighty nice to have some young people around. Perhaps it would be wiser to try to find out why children are rebellious, and avoid the causes.

Over a ten-year period, Drs. Eleanor and Sheldon Glueck studied 1000 boys. Five hun-dred were persistent delinquents, and 500 nondelinquents. Some interesting facts emerged: Of the delinquents, 96.9% came from unintegrated homes; 75.9% were hostile toward their fathers, and 86.2% were hostile toward their mothers. Whether the homes were broken by emotional tensions, death, or divorce, the children had been deprived of affection, security, social opportunities, and physical necessities; but, most of all a sense of belonging. Many of them sought to fill those needs through joining a delinquent gang.

Police records have revealed for many years that more than 70 percent of all juvenile delinquents come from broken homes, and that the rate is much higher in homes broken by divorce than by death. When parents rebel against the sanctity of marriage (Matt. 19:6), how can they expect children deprived of a normal home, the affection of father or mother--or both, emotional, financial, and social security, not to be rebellious?

God has given some precious promises that good parents can claim. He has promised that if we train up a child in the way he should go, when he is old he will not depart from it (Prov.

22:6). Notice God did not promise a child would never rebel under even the best of circumstances. Dealing with rebellious children usually brings us closer to the Lord. We come to understand how God feels when His children rebel against Him.

Parents are commanded to bring children up in the nurture and admonition of the Lord (Eph. 6:4). And teaching is not *training*.

Parental influence is much like stereophonic sound. If the two speakers harmonize, the result is pleasant. If they are discordant, the sound is irritating, and we turn it off. This is what children do to parents who disagree in front of them.

Children must have love if they are to develop the best that is in them. And God is love (Deut. 6:6-9; 8:1-3; Job. 23:12; II Tim. 3:14-17). Remember the Lord's first command is: "Thou shalt love. . ."

Love is not automatic; it is a learned experience. Children learn to love their parents exactly the same way we learn to love God: because He first loved us (I John 4:19).

If you cannot love your children enough to at least endure your mate so the little ones can get a decent start in life, you don't love them much–or God at all (I John 4:20-21). After all, your children did not choose your mate–you did. Is it fair to leave them with someone you can't tolerate? Or if you are the "good " parent, is it fair to deny them your society? Is that practicing the Golden Rule? (Matt. 7:13).

Any time we fail to love one another, we disobey God's specific command (I John 3:2324). The ability to love does not come naturally; it is an achievement we have to work on all our lives. And we need not expect to perfect our aim this side of heaven (Psa. 17:15). We don't have to like our companion or our children; we only have to love them. Remember we like people because. . .; we love them in spite of. . . .

When children are brought up to love and obey God (and the only way to do that is by example), we have God's promise that they will eventually turn out all right. They may, however, break our hearts in the meantime.

Sending children to church or Sunday School one hour or two a week is far from bringing them up in the nurture and admonition of the Lord. Even if parents *take* them faithfully to all the teaching, training, and worship services of their church, then go home and have "roast preacher" for lunch, it's not likely to increase the children's admiration for God, their parents, or the church.

Unless children receive daily religious training in the home by precept and example, public worship may do them more harm than good. Children hate hypocrisy. God's instructions are to teach them about the Lord every day as we go about our daily lives (Deut. 6:4-9). We cannot expect children to be more dedicated to God than their parents are. Whatever consistent example we set before them, we can be reasonably certain they will follow.

Parents who smoke, drink, carouse, and live on medicine (drugs) can expect their children to do likewise. When parents lie and cheat, they need not expect to bring up honest children. Whatever goals the parents set, the children will probably set the same—unless the goals are so disgustingly radical or unrealistic that they go in the opposite direction.

Even sincere Christian parents are sometimes so "salty" their children rebel in disgust. And occasionally, children of ungodly parents get so ashamed of their elders that they rebel by turning to God. But as a rule, whatever the parents are, the children will be more of-good or bad.

God has given us many directions for rearing our children; we ignore them at the risk of our serenity, and our children's souls. Good parents usually aspire to leave their children a nice inheritance. What richer legacy can parents ever leave them than a good name? Solomon said, "A good name is rather to be chosen than great riches. . ." (Prov. 22:1). Who was better qualified to know?

If you leave your children houses, lands, stocks, bonds, or bank accounts, they may all be lost, stolen, or destroyed. A good name can only self-destruct. A good name, of course, is the fruit of good character. You cannot give your children character, but you can by your example inspire them to develop their own. And character is the one thing acquired in this world that you can take with you into the next.

We have God's promise that whatever we sow, we shall also reap (Gal. 6:7). We are prone to think of that inexorable law only in terms of punishment for our sins. But it applies to our good deeds as well. If parents strive always to obey the laws of God and man in private as well as in public, they can claim God's promise to have law-abiding children.

Let's not forget, however, that God's first command is to love. If our obedience to God is a chore (and if it is, the children will know), and if we fail to discipline our children with kindness and love, they are not likely to find service to God attractive, or feel other than rebellious toward us.

Parents are a child's first contact with authority. If they do not merit the children's respect, and secure implicit submission to their own authority, they cannot expect them to submit to the authority of teachers, police, or the ultimate authority: God. As a rule, people feel toward God when they are mature exactly as they felt toward their parents as little children. If they love and trust their parents, loving and trusting God comes naturally.

Parents should be kind, but firm and consistent in their discipline. Obedience should be established as a principle and wrought as a habit. Submission should be secured by means that it can be rendered cheerfully. A child should always know that any punishment he receives is for his own good, never to relieve his parents' irritation.

Parents are advised to chasten children when they need it (Prov. 13:24), but they are also admonished against provoking them to wrath (Eph. 6:4). Parents cannot *command* their children's respect; they have to earn it. And God has provided ample opportunity for parents to earn a child's respect and his implicit obedience. Remember that long period of weak and dependent infancy?

Animals leap quickly from weakness to strength, and from helplessness to self-reliance. Human babies mature slowly, giving parents many valuable years to mold their little minds into obedience and virtue. This is the most awesome responsibility God has given to parents; it cannot be relegated to anyone else without loss to both parents and children. Babysitters replace parents at the peril of the children, parents, and society.

During the earliest development of a child's moral consciousness, parents occupy the place of God in many vital respects. To the infant mind, they are the ultimate authority. Even if left with a babysitter, the child's ideas of a higher Power are father and mother. If he gets the impression there is a supreme power, a beneficient love, which becomes to him the fountain of all good, it is his parents.

To the pre-school child, parents are (or ought to be) the perpetual presence that later he should come to recognize as God. Therefore, the development of his sense of obligation to obey, and his dawning concept of rightful authority are their responsibility.

In the light of these eternal truths, it is essential for parents to establish in a child's mind as perfect a concept as possible of the true God, if they do not want their children to rebel against His authority and theirs. It is the parent's duty to make certain that no willfully wrong deeds or temper tantrums on their part are responsible for giving their children erroneous concepts of the Father in heaven.

All the vital relationships of a child to his parents are involved in a child's relationship to God. It is, therefore, the parents' solemn duty to make certain that disobedience to rightful authority never becomes a habit by being allowed to pass uncorrected.

Submission to parental authority, if properly taught, provides the only foundation that will support conformity to the laws of God and man as the child grows to adulthood. Anyone who is allowed to get away with rebellious behavior as an infant will likely rebel against whoever and whatever displeases him all his life.

You can interrupt the building of a road, and ten years later pick up and go on about where you left off. But if you neglect proper rearing of your children for ten years, and then try to assume your responsibilities, you can by no means begin where you left off. Your children will be irreparably grown up–enemies and liabilities to you and to society instead of friends and assets.

If you did fail to properly love and discipline your infant, and you already have a rebel, what now? Is there any hope?

With God, all things are possible (Matt. 19-26); He is not out of miracles.

Are you willing to do what God demanded of His people at the Jordan: Get right with Him yourself? Then ask God and the rebellious child to forgive you and sacrifice everything in your own life that is contrary to the laws of God. When you meet the conditions in Matt. 6:33 and John 15:7, you can claim the promises.

Granted, it will take a miracle to reclaim a rebellious child. But when you live in obedience to God, you can expect miracles.

The proper rearing of children is parents' first duty to God. But you do have to make a living for them, too. Do you need a few miracles in that area?

Doesn't Anybody Care?

Chapter 8

YOUR WORK

Life is composed primarily of three compartments: the emotional (home and family), physical (health and vocation), and spiritual (God and church). To be happy and well-adjusted, one needs to function happily in all three areas. You can get along fairly well, however, with two compartments functioning. You can survive if you have a happy relationship in only one. But anyone who loses all three, is almost certain to suffer a mental, physical, or emotional breakdown.

One who has no church relationship (or an unhappy one) is minus one third of the joy in life already. An unhappy home situation leaves only work. Many people work with fervent zeal at their vocations because work is their whole existence.

Home and family, and church are usually the most important elements in the happy person's life, but work is vitally important also.

One cannot be happy who makes no contribution to the world. The ditch digger and the scrub woman can rest in pride at the end of the day, because they have contributed to the welfare of their fellow man. The professional playboy's eternal quest for pleasure ends only in frustration because he is always taking-never giving. "Work in heavy doses will cure nine out of ten neuroses."

What are the big problems with your work? Inadequate compensation? Obnoxious co-workers? Unsuitable vocation? What can you do?

Everyone should find a vocation, which is not work–to him. "Work," said a little boy, "is what other people think of for you to do. Play is what you think of for yourself."

The born homemaker never thinks of the washing, ironing, mending, cooking and cleaning as menial labor; it is simply her opportunity to keep her beloved family comfortable.

The farmer, who loves the soil and living, growing things, puts in at least eighteen hours a day six or seven days a week during his busiest season. He doesn't think of it as slave labor, however, be he ever so tired; he enjoys every day of it. And he is frequently the lowest paid on the national financial scale. If the farmer's family income was figured on a wage-hour basis, he would always be at the bottom of the list.

But what is the ambition of many bankers, college professors, and other professional people? To retire on a little farm; they think of it as the nearest thing to heaven. And they are probably right.

If anyone works longer hours than the farmers, it is the divinely-called preachers and teachers. Seldom does the chosen minister think of his vocation as work at all, but a privileged place of service.

Teachers, who love people and delight in sharing knowledge with them, often feel guilty at taking money for doing something they enjoy so much. Their most devoted friends are usually numbered among their former students.

Many public-school teachers, however, don't dare park their cars at the school lest they find their tires flat at the end of the day–often slashed. Such teachers are in the wrong profession.

Teachers who love their students can park their cars anywhere–unlocked. If a student touches the car at all, it is usually to leave a gift of fruit, flowers, or a favorite book or poem.

The teaching and preaching professions have always been almost as poorly paid as farming, yet there is seldom a shortage in either field. The divinely called ones will preach and teach even if they have to work at something else to make a living.

And it is the same with the carpenter who takes pride in his building; the merchant who cherishes his merchandise; the salesman who delights in selling, and all the other professions.

Even the unskilled in the most menial work should enjoy being able to support their families, and contribute to the nation's economy and the welfare of the world. Any productive work should bring joy to somebody with a talent for that kind of task.

So how do you find the vocation that is not toil–but joy? First meet the conditions and claim the promises in Prov. 3:1-6. Then, because we live in a very real and practical world, and God will not do anything for you that you can do for yourself, you should seek out the best counseling and testing center available, and listen to professional advice. If the experts advise you to change vocations, it would probably be wise to consult your financial advisor, talk with your pastor, and confide in one or two close friends who are familiar with your situation and the vocation you are considering.

If, however, the consensus of friends and experts is that you should stay where you are, and you get no leadership from God to do otherwise (the Holy Spirit often leads us through the counsel of Christian friends), then check further for the source of your discontent.

Do you feel you are underpaid? If so, make every effort to increase your productivity. All you have to do is increase your skill to the limit of your ability, and then claim God's promise in Luke 6:38.

Are you unhappy with your co-workers? If so, moving is seldom the answer. People are much the same wherever you go. You probably cannot change your associates much, but you can do wonders with yourself. Wherever you move, you take your faults along. It would be simpler to get rid of them right where you are. Even though you may have your worst enemies around you, your dearest friends are probably there, too. If you leave one, you leave the other. Few things contribute more to emotional maturity and Christian growth than roots and stability. Be certain God is leading before you decide to move on.

But whether you go or stay, claim the promise in Prov. 16:7. "When a man's ways please the Lord, he maketh even his enemies to be at peace with him." God never promised we would not have enemies-even Jesus had enemies, who were not satisfied until they killed Him. But He did promise that if we do that which pleases Him, He will make our enemies leave us alone. Eventually, they left Jesus alone (after He had fulfilled His Father's commands). There is no record of a single enemy lifting voice or hand against Him after the Resurrection. Jesus walked the earth for forty days before the Ascension; apparently, only His friends actually saw Him, but there is little doubt His enemies knew He was around.

There are several things we can do to make our ways please the Lord. We are advised in Prov. 15:1 that a soft answer turns away wrath, but grievous words stir up anger. Don't allow your associates to needle you into angry rebuttals. Remember that anger rests in the bosom of fools (Ecc. 7:9). Don't let your co-workers make a fool of you. Claim God's promise in Prov. 25:21-22. Don't be ostentatious about it; simply be humble and kind. Those are virtues that are most difficult to resist.

Conduct yourself wisely and charitably with others, but also be charitable with yourself. Remember, God said you were to love your neighbor as you love yourself. People who are self-deprecating and always apologizing for their very existence are depressing. No one is likely to think much more of you than you think of yourself, but if you make your work important, and your associates comfortable, it's quite likely they will return the favor.

Read carefully and prayerfully Ecc. 7:13-20, and as you strive to meet the conditions and claim the promises, remember that no one is perfect–neither you nor your associates. It could be that you are expecting too much, either of yourself, your fellow workers, or both. Even God does not expect perfection of any man, so why should you? We are "pilgrims and strangers here"; we must wait till we get to our home in heaven for perfection.

One of the favorite admonitions of Jesus is often ignored–or at least misapplied in many of our relationships. Jesus said, "It is more blessed to give than to receive" (Acts 20:35). Frequently, we take this to mean we should do all the giving, and we smother our friends and loved ones with gifts and services. But if you do all the giving, you get all the blessings. You may actually harm or antagonize the recipients of your gifts.

We have only to observe the bitter, rebellious army of welfare recipients to be convinced that giving to others does not always make them happy. God set the example for our conduct with each other. He will do nothing for us that we can do for ourselves. He fed the children of

Israel with manna from heaven for forty years while they were in the desert where no food was available. But the first day after they arrived in Canaan where food was plentiful, the manna ceased.

If you attempt to do a kindness for an enemy, you will likely be rebuffed. But if you ask him to do you a favor, he will probably do it. Don't deprive your associates, whether family, friends, or enemies, of the joy of doing things for you. There is a grace of receiving as well as a grace of giving. If everyone refused to receive, there could be no giving.

We enjoy giving gifts to children because they receive them so joyfully. Are you careful to accept gifts and services from others with joyous gratitude? Or do you reject gifts, and do all the giving yourself? If you do, you probably keep busy resenting the ingratitude of others.

You don't want to be a sponge, of course; nor do you want to be a doormat; neither are very high on the list of prized household articles. We simply use them and throw them away. But if you enjoy giving to others, then share your blessings by allowing them to do something for you.

The child who brings his mother a wilted bouquet of wild flowers will probably get greater joy out of her proudly putting them in a pretty vase and placing them on the mantle, than he will out of the most expensive toy she could bring him. It is always more blessed to give than to receive.

Perhaps your poor personal relationships are caused by your trying to do all the giving. Make a point of asking a favor of the associates you can't get along with, and see if your relationship does not improve.

Work, however, of any kind, demands reasonably good health. Do you need a miracle in that department?

Chapter 9

YOUR HEALTH

The relative value of health and wealth usually depends on which one you have lost.

With your health, as with other desired objectives, every promise God made is contingent upon your meeting the conditions. In Deut. 7:11-15, God promised His people every blessing they could possibly want if they would only obey Him. One of the blessings He promised was to take away "all sickness," So if you want good health, meet God's conditions.

And part of our obedience to God is taking care of our bodies. We need to be careful for the spiritual and moral as well as the physical well-being of our bodies. Several of the best diagnosticians agree that at least ninety percent of our physical ills have emotional bases.

Dr. John A. Schindler, M.D. in his *How to Live 365 Days a Year,* said that emotionally induced illnesses were more common than all the other diseases combined.

The fact that allergies, hay fever, asthma, arthritis, and ulcers are usually the result of prolonged stress or emotional tension is another recent discovery. But God's word has always advised happiness and humility as a source of good health (Prov. 16:18-24; 17:22).

God will forgive your sins as soon as you

repent; your nervous system is not so generous.

There is no question about the damage that moral debauchery does to the body (I Cor. 6:9-20). That is one problem the consecrated, obedient Christian does not incur. Unfortunately, however, many sincere Christians abuse their bodies in other ways. Improper diets, whether you eat too little, too much, or foods detrimental to health, are a sin against the body.

Overwork, lack of exercise, too little sleep–or too much–damages the body.

Frequently, mental patients are merely kept under sufficient sedation to produce restful sleep for about three days after their admittance to the hospital. Many times that is all the patient needs; after three days rest he is able to go back home and go to work.

Every adult with normal intelligence knows that nutritious food, regular exercise, and eight hours sleep are all essential to good health. To deprive your body of any one of the three is to invite ill health. It is also a sin (James 4:17).

Medical doctors have only recently discovered that eating fat meat is harmful to human health. God commanded His people not to eat it centuries ago. (Lev. 7:23).

Modern doctors report that alcohol is the biggest health problem in America. God commands us to leave it alone (Prov. 23:29-35; 20:1). Alcoholism has never yet afflicted anyone who does not drink alcohol. If it is a disease, it's the only one on record that men can-and do-buy in a bottle and deliberately inflict upon themselves.

If you want good health, it is no more likely to be yours with no effort on your part than is wealth, happiness, friends, or any other blessing. But, again, God will not do for you what you can do for yourself. It is utterly useless to ask God to give you good health while you continue to abuse your body.

A young mother of four preschool children suffered from migraine headaches. They became so severe she spent at least one day a week in the hospital under heavy sedation. Her husband, an auto mechanic, eventually could no longer carry the load-physically, financially, or emotionally. The wife consulted a marriage counselor who took her to the best internist available.

When the doctor learned the young mother was under the care of the most reputable neuro-surgeon in the area, and that he found nothing organically wrong, he refused even a glance at the large stack of x-rays she brought with her. He said, "If Dr.Ellis says there's nothing wrong with your head, I'm sure there isn't. Now let's look elsewhere for your trouble."

When the internist learned the woman was living on coffee and cigarettes, and trying to survive on about four hours of broken sleep at night, he wrote out two prescriptions: one for some tablets to take if she felt a headache coming on; the other for a new way of life. He prescribed *no* coffee or cigarettes, eight hours sleep at night plus a thirty-minute nap in the afternoon, and three nourishing meals a day to include meat, milk, fruit, bread, vegetables, and cereals.

The doctor cautioned his patient to be sure she took what he prescribed, and be equally sure she took nothing else–not even an aspirin.

She followed the doctor's directions to the letter–not because she wanted to, but because she stood to lose everything she held dear if she could not regain her health. She never had another migraine. Her nervousness, and marital problems also disappeared. As an added bonus, all four children got rid of their allergies.

Many Christians, who would not dream of abusing their bodies with cigarettes or alcohol, think nothing of eating themselves into a mountain of fat and an early grave. Gluttony is a sin that the Scriptures equate with drunkenness (Deut. 21:18-21; Prov. 23:21).

When a vastly overweight preacher waddles into the pulpit, whatever message he may have is already lost on the majority of his congregation. How can he admonish others to obey the laws of God when he refuses to do so?

Many fat people deceive themselves by insisting their weight is the result of a glandular malfunction. If it really is, why not have it corrected as one would any other body deficiency? The obese may deceive themselves, but they rarely deceive anyone else.

Overeating is disobedience to God just as much as drinking and moral debauchery, and it nearly as detrimental to the body. In one way gluttony is even more damaging to a Christian's witness than any of the other seven deadly sins. Who can tell by looking at a stranger that he is a drunkard, a liar, a thief, or a lecher? But people can spot a glutton as far as they can see him.

It's no sin for a man to enjoy good food. Neither is it a sin for him to admire a pretty woman; but if she belongs to another man, God commands him to leave her alone. And disobedience to the commandments of God is sin. Intemperance is a lust of the flesh whether it is drinking, carousing, or overeating (Gal. 5:16-24).

The obvious fact that obesity is so very detrimental to one's health should be sufficient evidence that it is wrong. Any abuse of our bodies is sin.

A Greek proverb says, "Whom the gods would destroy they first make opulent–then corpulent."

If we want to serve God, Paul admonishes us to lay aside every weight and every sin that hinders us. Anything that damages our health is a hindrance to God's service, and that includes working ourselves to exhaustion. Much of the apathy and turmoil in our churches is the direct result of Christians being too sick or too tired to serve the Lord acceptably. That, too is sin (Rom. 12:1-2).

Turmoil in our churches always begins with turmoil in individual hearts. The trouble in your church may arise from a source quite different than you think.

Chapter 10

TURMOIL IN THE CHURCH

The church must be a very strong and righteous thing, for it has survived every enemy it ever had.
—Eddie Cantor

Within every heart, the Creator has reserved a space for Himself. Either God will fill it, or it will become a vacuum. If one third of your life is empty, you are severely handicapped.

During the first dispensation, God the Father manifested Himself to individuals through the family (Abraham, Isaac, and Jacob). During the second dispensation, God the Son manifested Himself directly to individuals (Peter, James, and John). During this third and last dispensation, God the Holy Spirit reveals Himself to individuals through the Church. Remember the Revelation Christ gave to John on Patmos was sent to the Churches.

Paul said be glory to God "in the Church by Christ Jesus throughout all ages, world without end" (Eph. 3:14-21). How many people do you know who have found God, who found Him some other way than through the Church? It may have been through the preaching, teaching, or healing ministry, a gospel tract, the witness of an individual member or even the silent testimony of the virtuous life of a humble Christian, but it still came through a church.

God uses people to promote His kingdom. He has chosen to unite them in organizations called churches. Destroy the churches, and you destroy the only vehicles God has to bring people into His kingdom. The church cannot be destroyed from without; it can only self-destruct.

Some member's disobedience to God is always at the root of turmoil in a church. That much is usually obvious. Just whose disobedience may not be so obvious.

You are probably saying, "Now wait just a minute! Isn't Satan to blame for trouble in the church?"

But doesn't Satan usually work through some of the members? Remember Judas Iscariot? He was not a saved person-but he was a member of the original church.

Some fifty years ago in a pioneer country church, the young pastor preached a sermon on divorce. He made it pretty plain that he and the Lord were both against it.

Apparently, the sermon caused scarcely a ripple of anything except amens. The majority of those hard-working frontiersmen thought the only difference between divorce and disgrace was in the spelling.

But soon after that sermon a whispering campaign began. Nobody seemed to know just who started it, but the gist of it was that the church was not progressing as it ought. True it had grown phenomenally during its brief three years, and almost every family in the community attended regardless of their religious conviction. But there were still some hardened old sinners and a few wild young bucks who had not walked the sawdust trail.

"Perhaps if we had a new pastor. . ." the whispers invariably ended.

A saintly looking deacon with flowing white locks and a long white beard decided it was his Christian duty to inform the pastor about the gossip. The pastor resigned immediately. It was not his first church, but he was its first pastor. The little church fell apart. In more than fifty years, while that little community has doubled in population many times, that church has not regained the attendance nor the spirit it had those first three years.

The pious old deacon, who loved to preach anyway, offered to take over as pastor. In the ensuing discussion it came to light that the deacon's first two wives divorced him! All the neighbors heard about were the last two who died.

The truth also emerged as to who started the whispering campaign. It seemed that deacon was convinced the Lord didn't approve of the pastor preaching against the deacons.

When the pastor, deacons, Sunday School superintendent, or whoever, take the stand that opposing their leadership or conduct is opposing the Holy Spirit, it doesn't do much for the spirit of the church.

It's true that dissension in the church indicates there is "sin in the camp." But dissension in itself does not necessarily point out the sinners.

Caleb and Joshua were the only two dissenting members of that congregation of some two million. They were alone in supporting Moses and Aaron when they tried to lead the children of Israel into the promised land some two years after they left Egypt.

But it so happened those two lonely dissenters were right. And they were the only ones God permitted to live to cross the Jordan thirty-eight years later.

It takes more than the obedience of one or two people, however, to cure the trouble in a church. The church is a body. If one little finger gets smashed, the whole body suffers with it. But as long as head, neck, and backbone are sound, a body can function productively. (Remember Ann Adams, the artist who is confined to an iron lung by polio? She draws fantastic pictures with a pencil in her mouth.) But when a head fails to function properly the rest of the body is not worth much.

The pastor is the earthly head of the church. A pastor does not have to be a moral degenerate, a thief, or a fool to ruin his church. If he is arrogant, self-righteous, or dictatorial, the people will not follow him–even when he is right about the things he tries to do.

Sheep ranchers are reputed to be uncooperative church workers. One old fellow explained it this way. "You people amuse me. You have all kinds of schemes, papers, and discussions on ways to get people to come to your meetings. I never heard a word at a sheep meeting on how to get sheep to come to the troughs. We put all our time in on the best kind of feed."

God compared His people to sheep-never cattle. Sheep must be gently led by someone they trust, and they are very particular about what they eat. The leader may even be a member of their own flock, but led they must be; they cannot be driven like cattle. A member of the flock, however, cannot feed and protect them; only a shepherd can do that. Sheep without a shepherd usually drift aimlessly and helplessly to eventual destruction.

The restoration of Jerusalem began with a great revival. It started when the preacher (Ezra) confessed his sins to God and before the people. The congregation joined their leader in repentance. Immediately they began to put away their sins, and live in obedience to God. Then God blessed them with His healing power. The people courageously rebuilt their city, the wall, and their lives.

It's true if the preacher will fill the people, the people will fill the pews. However, Christians should not stay away from church just because the preacher can't preach. Fervent prayers from faithful members might do wonders for his sermons. In fact, we should never stay away from church for any reason we could not conscientiously give our Maker.

No church ever progresses beyond its pastor's leadership. That does not mean every time a church flounders, the pastor needs to move.

Preachers can get right with God without moving just the same way the membership can.

There is little doubt that a penitent, obedient church could bring about a miraculous change in the leadership. Just a few consecrated, praying people can bring down God's power (Matt. 18:20). But without Godly leadership it is difficult to unite even a few people in prayer.

It is doubtful if there is ever an entire church united in obedience to God. Sometimes there are members so bold and stubborn in their wickedness they will have to be removed before the church can function effectively. Doesn't a human body have to undergo radical surgery sometimes to survive? If a member of your body has cancer or gangrene, that member has to go if you are to live. But radical surgery is done only after every effort has been made to save the infected member. The same policy needs to apply to the members of our churches.

For a church to lop off its head is suicide as surely as it is for a a human body. Only God can replace a head and make it work. If you feel your church needs a new head, perhaps it does. Then again it could be you who needs changing. Ask the Lord about it.

God holds the pastors in His hand (Rev. 1:20). Ask Him to take care of the pastor, and remove him or keep him according to His will. But before you are ready to pray effectively about the pastor, you need to be sure your own house is in order. Are you doing your best to live in complete obedience to God? If you are, and you can get a few more consecrated people to join you in prayer, God will take care of the pastor-whether he goes or stays. And when the leadership gets right with God, the flock is sure to follow.

God placed the church in the world like you put a boat into the water; that's where it belongs. Take a boat out of the water, and it will eventually dry up and fall apart. But if the water gets into the boat, it sinks immediately. So it is with the church; it has to be in the world or it can't give service. But if the world gets into the church it's sunk. Do you need a miracle to get the world out of your church? You can't bring the whole body into obedience, but you can start with one member.

Some men excuse themselves for not attending public worship by faithfully sending their families. "Church," they say, "is for women and children."

It is true there are more women in church than men. It's also true there are more men in jail than women.

A little boy expressed a sentiment on church attendance, men might profitably emulate:

Each time I pass a church,
I stop to make a visit
So that when I'm carried in
Our Lord won't say, "Who is it?"

Service to God may begin with public worship, but even the most faithful church attendance cannot fulfill our responsibilities to God. We need to take God's message to the unchurched.

The only way we can take the church into the world is by fellowshipping with our neighbors. No one can cheat, abuse, or ignore his neighbor all week and expect to enjoy sweet fellowship together at church on Sunday. And singing "There's a Sweet, Sweet Spirit in This Place" does not necessarily make it so.

But suppose your neighbor is obnoxious?

Chapter 11

OBNOXIOUS NEIGHBORS

A Danish proverb says, "No one is rich enough to do without a neighbor."

There is probably no Scripture in all the Bible with which man is more familiar than "Thou shalt love thy neighbor. . ." And probably none is violated more frequently.

One of the most beloved and familiar parables of Jesus is that classic illustration of showing love for a neighbor: The Good Samaritan. The Samaritan ministered to the down-and-outer, whom others ignored. He offered his services freely without any expectation of reward. He went the second mile by continuing to show concern for the victim after he was safely at the inn.

There is another facet to that story, however, that is seldom emphasized: The man who fell among thieves was grateful and cooperative. When the victim was patched up and safely astride the donkey, he did not kick his benefactor in the teeth and ride off with the beast.

Because God commands us to love our neighbor, many a charitable Christian has paid with his life for picking up a hitchhiker, stopping to help a "stranded" motorist, or opening his door to strangers in the night. Has the Bible nothing to say about that sort of thing?

It does indeed.

If God had intended that we base all our conduct on one verse of Scripture, He would only have given us one. But He gave us many Scriptures. And Paul said, "All Scripture is given by inspiration of God, and is profitable for doctrine, for reproof, for correction, for instruction in righteousness" (II Tim. 3:16).

We live in a realistic world, and we have a realistic God who knows that some of our neighbors are obnoxious. What did He say about them? He said several things; one was "forsake the foolish and live, and go in the way of understanding" (Prov.9:6). Jesus said, "Cast not your pearls before swine" (Matt. 7:6). God commended the church at Ephesus because they could not bear them that were evil (Rev. 2:2), and He condemned the church at Thyatira because they tolerated evil Jezebel to work among them (Rev. 2:18-23).

Loving your neighbor does not mean you have to approve his evil conduct, nor that you have to accept him as a bosom companion. It means you will do him no harm, and you will do him good if possible.

The Bible says when our ways please the Lord, He makes even our enemies to be at peace with us (Prov. 16:7). But God knows the only way to have peace with some people is to avoid them. When you have humbly and sincerely tried every way you know to get along with a neighbor, and he has repaid you with treachery, torment, and slander, your only choice as a peacemaker or a good neighbor is to leave him alone. And God says do just that (Prov. 9:6-7).

Jesus commanded His disciples to depart from the people who rejected them, and to shake the very dust off their feet–severing the relationship completely (Matt. 10:11-15).

Just because somebody hates you does not necessarily mean you have failed to love your neighbor. Naboth had done no wrong, yet he was convicted of capital crimes in a legal court of law, and stoned to death. His only crime was refusing to give up his property to his neighbor who coveted it (I Kings 21:1-16).

Jesus loved everybody, and never did any harm to a living soul, yet so many people hated Him with such passion that they slandered Him, beat and abused Him, and eventually managed to get Him executed–by legal authorities.

The Master warned His disciples that He would be killed for obeying His Father, and they would be killed for following Him. Contrary to people hating you being evidence that you have failed to love your neighbor, Jesus cautioned His followers they were certain to be out of the will of God when *all* man spoke well of them (Luke 6:26). Strict obedience to God always makes some people hate you. The best way, however, to get rid of an enemy is to make him a friend.

We all encounter a few people with whom we cannot have fellowship. But if you can't live peaceably with anybody, you can be sure there is something wrong with you. If you want to be happy, humbly and sincerely try to find out what your problem is. Your pastor or a Christian counselor can help you. Even a devout Christian friend or relative might help you solve your problem.

The most important thing, of course, is to be sure our ways please God. Many times we are forced to choose between pleasing God, and pleasing our neighbors. If you choose to please your neighbors, remember you must give an account to God for all disobedience to Him (Rom. 14:12). We are not accountable to our neighbors for our conduct–only to God. As long as you and God know you love your neighbor, and have tried your best to get along with him, and do the right thing, you will eventually come out all right. You may, of course, have to wait til you get to heaven for vindication.

You are not accountable to your neighbors in the final judgment, but they very well may take you to account in this world–and convict you. They convicted Jesus of evil doing, and He said the servant is not above His Lord (Matt. 10:21-26).

There is only one thing worse than obnoxious neighbors, and that is obnoxious relatives. Do you need a miracle with your relatives–especially your in-laws?

Chapter 12

MEDDLING IN-LAWS

Preceded only by money and sex, meddling in-laws are blamed more frequently than anything else for breaking up marriages. Couples who abide by God's instruction for establishing a new home are not likely to have in-law trouble.

First of all, God said leave father and mother (Gen. 2:24). If every bride and groom would put at least 500 miles between them and their nearest relatives, they would eliminate almost every opportunity for in-law meddling.

It is most difficult for good parents with the best of intentions to keep their mouths shut while their grown-up children make foolish mistakes.

A girl from a poor, hardworking, conservative family married and settled down in the city where her parents lived. She had a good job; her husband had a good job, and they owed no one. They saw no reason, with their combined incomes, they should not live well. They promptly bought a new house, car, television, stereo, and early American furniture.

The bride's parents tried to keep quiet, but with every purchase they grew more frantic. They advised, pleaded, and eventually scolded the newlyweds. They tried to tell them all the possibilities that their installment buying could involve. Relationships became strained, uncomfortable, and finally they were severed. The young couple ceased to visit the parents, and made it quite plain the parents were not welcome in their home.

The grieving elders alternated between berating themselves for meddling, and condemning their daughter for her stubborn foolishness.

In less than a year, however, the daughter called her mother and meekly asked if she could come home for a visit. The mother was almost beside herself with joy. But the parental joy was short-lived. When the girl arrived, she was obviously pregnant, and looked as if she had aged ten years. She said she had been forced to quit work because she was so deathly ill. Then her husband was drafted.

The money the army private was able to send home was insufficient even for living expenses and medical bills; there was none left for installment payments. The mortgage on the house had been foreclosed. The car had to go back tomorrow, and they were being sued on the furniture.

The parents were careful not to say "I told you so," but the daughter was so painfully aware of their thoughts they were like the invisible rabbit, Harvey, always between them.

Unable to help financially, all the parents could do was keep their sick daughter in their home and take care of her. And even there they could not protect her from bill collectors and process servers. They hounded her until she barely made it to the maternity ward before she landed in the psychiatric ward. Her mother took care of the baby.

Three years and three babies later, the father was home to stay, and the young couple began reconstructing their home. But that time they took a modest apartment furnished with "early family" furniture instead of early American.

If they had gone to a distant city when they married, they would have been just as foolish financially, but the parents would not have had to watch, suffer, and create emotional scars that will be forever sensitive. Following God's admonition to "leave father and mother" would have saved a lot of ill will.

Then there are other kinds of in-laws. There are possessive mothers who want nothing but their darlings back home. And possessive fathers who cannot bear to see their sons grow up and become independent of them. They advise and control until their children find it impossible to create lives of their own.

In addition to "leave father and mother," God also commanded man to "cleave" to his wife. When husband and wife cleave to each other, there is no space left for in-laws–or anyone else–to get between them. And no one can come between any couple unless they themselves create the vacancy.

Husbands and wives should be loyal to each other. One should not discuss the other's shortcomings with anyone except God and the offending mate. If you must have a human shoulder to cry on, it should be the pastor, a Godly marriage counselor, or a wise and consecrated Christian friend. Remember, God's word advises against the counsel of the ungodly (Psa. 1:1). However efficient they may be, God's children are disobedient to Him when they seek counsel of ungodly psychiatrists, psychologists, or friends.

If you need a miracle to solve your in-law problems, check carefully God's rules, and see if you have kept them. If you have already violated the rules, talk the situation over with God, your mate, and a Christian counselor, and start over–if you can–by God's rules.

Of course, when a young couple start out sincerely trying to abide by Matt. 6:33 and 7:12, they seldom have in-law trouble or any other problems they can't solve.

You can, as a rule, avoid many of your in-laws, but parents, at one time or another, must have your attention. What can you do about parents?

Chapter 13

PARENT PROBLEMS

The first real problems a child encounters are with his parents: They won't do what he wants them to do. Parents enjoy quoting the fifth commandment, "Honor thy father and thy mother. . .," but children prefer Eph. 6:4, ". . .fathers, provoke not your children to wrath:. . . ."

The teenager has next to the worst parent problems of anybody. Parents take practically all of the joy out of life throughout the teen years–and that is the longest span of anyone's life. After you reach twenty, the years begin to fly, and they fly faster every year. After you pass fifty, they go jet.

Actually, if it were not for the "unreasonable" restrictions parents impose on teenagers, the teens could be the most enjoyable period of life. They are the years one is discovering what life is all about. You find the world is not confined to your home and community, but it is a big, beautiful, wonderful place, with unlimited opportunities. There are wrongs, to be sure, but they only wait *your* generation's setting them right.

So what can you do with parents during those long, miserable, mixed-up years? Surely, only a miracle could get them off your back.

Parents are always bugging you to hang up

your clothes, clean your room, take out the garbage, and do something about your hair.

Well-you could hang up your clothes, clean your room, take out the garbage, and do something about your hair. This is obedience to God as well as your parents (Eph. 6:1-3). And remember it is obedience God requires before He can give you the miracle you need. Try meeting His conditions, and see if He does not supply the miracle.

After all, are you sure you can clean up the world if you can't even clean your own room? And you might do a better job of setting the world on fire if you practiced on the garbage. Most teenagers are sure they could run the school, the city, and the country better than the blind, stupid, prejudiced clods who have charge of it now; and perhaps you can. But a little practice in managing your parents would be valuable experience in learning to run the school, city, and country.

Reality is different to all of us; it depends on our frame of reference. The past is past, but what about the present and future? Your parents may be responsible for your past, but only you are responsible for your present and future.

As long as you are dependent on your parents financially, wouldn't it be the better part of discretion to at least try to cooperate with them? If they are smart enough to make a living for you, it is possible they may know more about some other things than you think they do.

It's true, you know, that your parents were once your age and felt just as repressed, rebellious, and capable as you do. They seem to have forgotten it by now, but then they have had several things to damage their memories. The struggles to pay bills, keep food on the table, and sit up with crying babies are powerful erasers.

But take courage; your prospects are bright. Once you get married, you will be free from parental restraint-provided you follow God's admonition to "leave" and "cleave." And if you do this, you should not have any more parent trouble for a while. In fact you can enjoy a fine friendship with them over the next twenty, thirty, or even forty years.

If your parents live to be old, however, you will probably think your teenage problems with them were child's play. "Old and childish" are usually inseparable words. What does it mean to be childish?

A child want what he wants when he wants it, and he does not care who it hurts. He isn't concerned that you are tired and sleepy; if he wants a drink in the middle of the night, he just yells. You accept that from your little ones as the way things are: cute, helpless, and sweet-at times. And after all, they will soon be grown up and won't need you any more.

Not so with your elderly parents. To watch beloved, respected adults who were once strong, wise, and kind, become weak, foolish, and cunningly cruel is bewildering and heartrending.

Regardless of how devoted, respectful, and obedient you have always been to your parents, if they live to become senile, the day will come when you can no more cater to their every whim than they could to you when you were a child.

If all parents were careful to treat their children with the same kindness, courtesy, and respect they want their children to extend to them if they should become old, helpless, and dependent guests in their homes, there would be far fewer rebellious children.

There are several tragic differences between taking care of helpless little children and helpless old parents. You can be patient with little children's unreasonable demands for several reasons: First, you expect them to grow up and cease to be unreasonable and demanding. And you don't have to give in to their demands; you can always spank them and tell them to be quiet.

Childish parents cannot be spanked.

You have no hope of your old parents getting better, either; you know they will get progressively worse as long as they live. And there is a vast difference between handling a twenty-pound child and a two-hundred pound adult in the bathing, feeding, and changing routines.

You have been your children's ages; you can empathize and understand. You have not been you parents' age; you can't possibly know how they feel. When your sainted mother can't walk across the floor without being supported on both sides, but she can zip out of bed to listen on the telephone extension, and get back before you can get to her, what do you do?

"Leave father and mother" was counsel given bride and groom-not middle-aged couples whose aged parents need their children more desperately than the children ever needed them. It may take several miracles to solve the problem of aged parents. For a start, you need to faithfully practice the Golden Rule.

Regardless of the time you spend looking after senile parents, you may have much longer to regret it if you don't take the best care of them possible. And while you are wondering how much more you can endure, claim God's promises in I Cor. 10:13. and I Peter 5:7.

Taking care of aged parents does not necessarily mean you have to take them into your home and personally minister to their needs. That could, in many cases, be more than you could bear, and that would violate God's promise not to suffer you to be burdened beyond endurance.

It is one thing for nurses to look after helpless, dependent, childish patients eight hours a day, and then go home to their families and forget the whole thing. It is quite another to turn a home into a hospital and be confined with a demanding patient twenty-four hours a day, seven days a week. It is also poles apart for an impersonal nurse to handle unreasonable, senile patients, and children to cope with senile parents. Old people usually take orders readily from nurses. From their own children? Never!

Modern miracle drugs, which prolong the lives of helpless old people beyond human dignity or decency, place almost as great a burden upon the children as they do on the aged parents. Before antibiotics, when old people got sick, they died. Now they can be kept alive almost indefinitely. Drugs that are a Godsend to the young can be a curse to the old. Until this problem is solved, you can only do your best, and trust God for the rest.

Just as good parents try to do the best they can for their little children, grown-up children can only do the best they can for aged parents. Faithfully obey Luke 6:38; Matt. 7:12; and John 15:7, and God will supply the miracle you need to survive. Taking care of your aged parents may not be easy, but was everything easy when they took of you?

But where do you get the time to make a living, cope with rebellious children, and take care of aged parents?

Chapter 14

THE ETERNAL BATTLE WITH TIME

Did you ever notice that people who have an hour to kill usually want to spend it with a friend who does not have a minute to spare?

Benjamin Franklin said, "Don't waste time, it is the stuff life is made of."

You can waste money-and earn more. You can waste food-and grow or buy more. You can waste water-and God will pour down more from the skies. But when you waste time-it is gone forever.

He who kills time has been likened to a murderer most foul.

People who think they need to kill time should try working it to death. Killing time is not really murder; it is actually suicide.

All the time we have is today. But today is often crucified between the two thieves of yesterday and tomorrow. Yesterday is gone. Tomorrow may never come. Today is all we are guaranteed. Be sure to use it well.

Are you one of that small minority who has more time than you need? If so, check Prov. 31:10-13 (if you are a woman), and see if you are looking well to the ways of your household. If you are a man, check Matt. 6:33, I Tim. 5:8, and Eph. 6:4.

Those who faithfully perform their duty to God, family, and neighbors, usually find they have joined the majority of people who never have time enough.

Even the old and infirm, or young but physically helpless, can stay busy praying for the needs of the world and the people around them–especially those who minister to their needs.

Time is an eternal mystery. God gives everyone exactly the same amount: twenty-four hours in each day. Yet time hangs so heavy on some people's hands they cannot endure it; they cut it short by suicide. Others never have enough time to do half the things they want to do–even though they may live a hundred years.

If you are the average person who needs a miracle to find time to do the things that must be done, what kind of obedience does God want from you before He can give you that miracle?

First of all, God wants you to be faithful in performing your duties to Him (Ex. 20:1-17, Matt. 6:33). Then He has promised to supply all your needs (Phil. 4:19).

If you sincerely attempt to perform your duties to God, family, and community, you will likely discover it will take a miracle just to find that much time (Eph. 5:15-16). Instead of hanging heavy on your hands, time becomes a priceless treasure.

You will also, of course, find Satan right there to resist your every effort for God (Zech. 3:1). Serving the Lord may not pay the greatest dividends in the world, but His retirement plan is fantastic!

To the busy earthling, one of heaven's most coveted assets is limitless time. If you are one of those busy people who hates to go to bed because you still have work to do, remember there will be no night in heaven (Rev. 2:25, 22:5).

True, you have all the time you want in heaven, but you will no longer have the opportunity to do the work that needed to be done on earth (Ecc. 9:9-10; Eze. 33:7-9).

God needs your service now. The world needs your ministry now. Society is in its present turmoil because God's watchman have not been vigilant in warning evil doers of the dire consequences of their wicked ways.

Why pay a psychiatrist to tell you not to feel guilty over failing to fulfill your responsibilities to God. It will cost far less in time and money to repent of whatver is making you feel guilty and miserable. Then thank God for His forgiveness, rectify whatever mistakes you can, forget the rest, and spend every day discharging as many of your responsibilities to God as possible. You will never again find time hanging heavy on your hands. God always has a solution.

If you are depressed and have no idea why, a Christian psychiatrist may be exactly what you need (Psa. 1:1). Consulting just any psychiatrist, however, might turn out like the fellow who was on his way to the top of the Empire

State Building to try to put an end to his misery. In the elevator he met a psychiatrist.

"Why do you want to kill yourself?" the doctor asked.

"Because life is not worth living. If it's not trouble with my wife and kids, it's problems with my job. Or it's bills. Bills! Bills! Always bills! And then there's the Internal Revenue!"

"Why don't you come into my office," coaxed the doctor, "and let's talk about it."

"Hold all calls," the doctor told his receptionist. "This man wants to jump out the window. He promised to give me one hour to convince him life is worth living."

When the hour was up and the doctor did not come out, the receptionist called him. He did not answer. There was no response to her knock on the door so she went in. They had both jumped.

An hour spent with a pessimist may not make you jump out a window, but wasted time always brings frustration and misery. Time well used is life itself, because time IS the stuff life is made of. One who has taken your time seldom recognizes it as a debt, yet it is the one debt he can never repay-the most hopeless debt of all.

Time is precious and it should be used like hoarded gold-very carefully. Here are ten ways to use your time wisely:

Take time to PRAY-prayer is the source of power.

Take time to THINK-thoughts are the source of wisdom.

Take time to WORK-it is not the nature of work but how well it is done that satisfies the soul.

Take time to LOVE-it is love that makes life worth living.

Take time to READ-reading is the fountain of knowledge.

Take time to GIVE-it is more blessed to give than to receive.

Take time to LAUGH-laughter is more healing than medicine.

Take time to be FRIENDLY-friends must be acquired BEFORE they are needed.

Take time to PLAY-play is the fountain of youth.

Take time to express GRATITUDE-sincere appreciation is the cream on the milk of human kindness.

Everyone has exactly the same amount of time: twenty-four hours every day. Used or wasted-it passes. A thirty-year-old marine veteran came into the counselor's office to withdraw from the university. "I can't stay here four years," he said. "Why in four years I'll be nearly thirty-five years old!"

"How old will you be in four years if you do not go to school?" the counselor asked.

The young man got the point. He graduated from the university, and became an outstanding football coach-something he had wanted to do as long as he could remember. Not everyone should spend four years in college, but if a college degree is essential to your goal in life, it is the best four years you can ever spend .

Life is an eternal conflict between the forces of good and evil. Time well spent is good; wasted time is a most destructive evil. The war waxes and wanes according to the strength, dedication, and determination of the combatants.

Peace and happiness come only when the forces for good are in power. And the forces for good never have enough time to minister to all those who need their services.

Idleness is wasted time, and it breeds guilt and evil. When the forces of evil are in control, the world is in chaos.

Is all right with your world, or do you need a miracle for your personal chaos?

Chapter 15

WORLD CHAOS

Many consecrated Christians are convinced only the Lord's return can solve the problems of the world. Even a cursory examination of history should assure us that there have been several times in the past when the world was much more wicked than it is now.

Most people can bear one kind of trouble at a time without folding up. Our problems usually result from trying to bear three: all the troubles we have now, all we ever had, and all we ever expect to have.

Troubles are like babies—they have to be nursed to grow and develop.

An anonymous poet wisely observed:

> If you talk about your troubles
> And tell them o're and o're,
> The world will think you like 'em
> And proceed to give you more.

Actually, trouble is the hot water that keeps us clean. If man had suffered no troubles millions of years ago, he would still be living in caves. And if he is not troubled over current world conditions, he may soon be back in the caves.

As Seneca said, "Gold is tried by fire, brave men by adversity."

If only the Christians who are vitally concerned about world conditions would claim

God's promise in II Chron. 7:14, we would get the miracle we need to change the universe.

But you say, "I'm only one person; what can I do?"

Queen Victoria was only one person, a lone woman in a man's world; but she changed England, and through England she exercised a cleansing influence on the entire civilized world.

"But she was a Queen with vast influence, " you say, "I'm nobody."

Wasn't it one lone woman, that you never heard of, who managed to get prayer and Bible reading banned from public schools in America? If one person can accomplish that much for Satan, couldn't another do as much for God?

At this very hour, parliaments are convening around the world to try to bring peace and harmony to this planet. The wisest statesmen can search the world over, and never find a better plan than the one proposed in Exodus 20.

It is not wrong to lie, steal, and kill just because God forbids it. It is wrong-that's why God said don't do it. Any time God forbids us to do anything, you can be sure His is trying to save us pain. Do parents forbid little children to play in the street only to exercise their authority?

If you want to make your home, church, community, or the world a better place, you need to start by making yourself a better person.

The pagan Chinese gave the world a proverb,
which Christian Americans would do well to
heed:

When there is righteousness in the heart,
There will be beauty in the character.
When there is beauty in the character,
There will be harmony in the home.
When there is harmony in the home,
There will be order in the nation.
When there is order in the nation,
There will be peace in the world.

If you really want to try to bring peace to the
world, you must begin with righteousness in
your own heart, and that calls for a miracle.
But righteousness begins with obedience to
God, and that starts with a willingness on your
part to try. Remember, God promises that *if* we
abide in Him, and His Word abides in us, we
can ask what we please, and it will be done
(John 15:7).

Of course, abiding in Him takes a bit of doing.
It also means we cannot ask anything displeasing
to God. And that eliminates a lot of things we
want. It also means you must do your best to
abide by the laws of God and man. Yes, that
includes obeying traffic laws, paying your
taxes, and serving on juries when called.

And when you serve on a jury, it means
upholding the law without allowing prejudice,
favor, or pity to obstruct justice. After all, it
was God who made the races, and one's color
should never influence a verdict. God also said

if a man kills, he should be killed. To condemn a murderer to death is obedience to God (Ex. 21:12-14)

Our modern society seems to be concerned only with the welfare of the criminals; God is concerned for the victims.

Professing Christians readily file suit against their brethren. This is diametrically contrary to God's law (Matt. 5:40-41; I Cor. 6:6-8).

God commands husbands to cherish their wives; wives to obey their husbands, and both to bring their children up in the nurture and admonition of the Lord (Eph. 6:4). Husbands and wives-both members of the same church-divorce each other, and orphan the children. Some wage bitter court battles over child custody; others abandon their offspring to whoever will take them in. It is debatable which process if further from "the nurture and admonition of the Lord."

Why blame God for the dissolution of society, while we tear it apart with our own hands? When mothers murder their own unborn children, what can we expect?

Granted, it would take several miracles to bring any kind of order out of the chaos of American society, but obedience must precede the miracles we need. First we have to get our own hearts right with God (be born into His family if we are not already His children). If you are God's child, you love Him. He says, "If you love me, keep my commandments" (John 14:15). So we must search the Scriptures to find what He wants us to do. For instance, Prov. 31:10-31 gives a complete summary of the duties of a Godly wife and mother.

When there is righteousness in your heart, it is evident to your companion, your children, and your associates. The Christian home should be a place of harmony and joyous living. If it is not, somebody in that home is not in the will of God. Any two people who will get right with God can get right with each other. The same applies to communities and nations.

When there is righteousness in the heart, there has to be beauty in the character. And when there is beauty in all the characters in the home, there will be harmony there. It is quite true, however, that it takes beauty in the characters of *all* the members of a home to produce harmony, but ugliness in the character of only *one* member of the home can turn it into a shambles.

The same is true in the church, community, state, nation, and the world. What hope have we, then, of ever having peace in the world? None. Jesus said there would be war and turmoil right up to the end of time (Matt. 24: 6-8). If that's the case, what's the point in trying?

Have you ever managed to achieve perfect righteousness in your own heart–or your home? Why haven't you given up there? The answer is simple, isn't it? The improvement you have made is well worth the effort. If that is true in your heart and home, would it not be equally worthwhile in your church, community, state, nation, and the world? But whether they are personal or national, if everyone practiced the Golden Rule, every controversy could be solved. It is impossible to have turmoil among individuals or nations when all parties concerned practice the Golden Rule.

None of us, however, are very objective about our own conduct. Can't you look back at some of the things that you did in all good conscience, and see now that the devil used you gloriously? You were certain you were following God's leadership, so how did it happen?

You were either carried away by your own emotions, or you followed your personal inclinations. It is easy to believe God is leading us to do something we want to do anyway. In that case, how can anyone be sure when God is leading?

We are physical, emotional, and spiritual. Regardless of the basic problem, however, if it is not solved, soon all three areas of our being become involved.

Conflict may make life interesting, but it rarely increases self-esteem. Mankind's universal ideal is peace. And God promises peace to all who trust in Him. "Thou wilt keep him in perfect peace, whose mind is stayed on thee: because he trusteth in thee. Isaiah 26:3.

So if the psychiatrists are right (and you are still in control of your emotions) you might improve your mental health more by going to work on the things that increase your selfesteem than by going to a hospital.

In describing a virtuous woman, Solomon said, "She looks well to the ways of her household, and eats not the bread of idleness" (Prov. 31:27). Is that the area in which you need to be obedient to receive the miracle you need to be happy?

You cannot depend on your natural inclinations–they are to do evil (Jer.17:9). You cannot depend on your feelings or emotions; they can be deceiving (II Thess. 2:9-12). The only things in this world you can depend on are: death, taxes, change, and the promises of God. But to claim the promises of God, you must meet His conditions. To understand those conditions, you must be able to "rightly divide the word of truth" (II Tim. 2:15).

One must be rational and mentally healthy to be able to "rightly" interpret the Word of God.

Are you mentally healthy? What we want most, of course, is to be happy. Physical health is a blessing, but many people do manage to be happy without it. Can you be happy, however, without mental and spiritual health?

Anyone who has ever suffered emotional or spiritual illness knows it is as real as a broken leg–and ten times as painful. Are you emotionally healthy? Or would it take a miracle to give you emotional health? You can never solve a problem until you are aware of what that problem is.

You may be convinced the world is black and lonely, and there is no hope for happiness anywhere. The truth may be, however, that only your world is black. Remember little Pippa in Browning's immortal poem? While she skipped through all kinds of misery and degradation, she sang, "God's in his heaven-All's right with the world." All was right with *Pippa's* world.

The mentally ill live in a black world all the time-no matter how bright the world may be around them. Do you need a miracle to bring you out of that black blanket of depression? If so, the first thing you need to recognize is that the problem may lie within you-not your surroundings.

All anyone wants is to be happy. What does it take to make you happy? Do you know? If you don't-you need to find out. If you do, what do you plan to do about it? Do you know how to get what you want?

When you visit your doctor, what's the first thing you want him to do after he examines you? You want him to tell you what's wrong with you-*if* you don't already know. Why? Because he has to find what's wrong before he knows what to do. And so do you.

Are you emotionally ill? If so, how do you plan to solve your problem?

Chapter 16

MENTAL HEALTH

The first symptom of mental illness is usually anhedonia: the total incapacity to feel any pleasant emotion. The most vital element in mental health, according to eminent psychiatrists, is self-esteem. But even lay persons are usually aware it is not what other people think of them that keeps them awake nights, but what they think of themselves.

A drab young woman in the advanced state of pregnancy walked into the university Counseling-Testing Center. "Can you help me," she asked. "If you can't, I'm going to kill myself."

The counselor assumed the student was unmarried, and could not cope with the situation. When she learned the woman was the wife of a prominent graduate student, and had a two-year-old daughter, she assured her she had much to live for. "Don't you realize your husband is a brilliant young man with a promising future?"

"He's not very smart or he would never have married me," she wept.

Several counseling sessions and numerous tests confirmed the counselor's suspicions that the girl's problem was the most common cause of neurotic depression–lack of self-esteem. The wife, like her husband, was almost a straight-A student. She had a bright, beautiful little girl, and a devoted mate, but her lack of self-esteem prevented her enjoying either of them.

When a healthy, talented, person lacks self-esteem it's obvious he has an emotional problem. But suppose he is totally devoid of talent and skill, whence comes self-esteem? What makes anyone of value?

The first question a good psychiatrist usually asks a new patient is: "Tell me who you are."

The answer desired but seldom received is: "I'm a child of The King." People who are aware they are children of God rarely need a psychiatrist. However, just as physicians get infections, even psychiatrists get depressions.

After listing the most coveted spiritual gifts, the apostle Paul said, "I'll show you a better way." And the quality Paul said surpasses all others is love. Love does not require talent, skill, nor training; its only essential is being nice.

George Burns, the 90-year-old award-winning actor said, "It takes just as much energy to be rotten as it does to be nice. And I'll tell you something else," Burns added, "When you put energy into being nice, you usually get back more than you give."

Try making a list of family and friends you love most. Then beside their names list their talents and skills. Is there any correlation between your affection for them and their native abilities? Perhaps you already knew you love them largely because they love you. If love endears others to you, is it not logical that love also endears you to them? So if love is our finest asset, our self-esteem should be based on our ability to love. How do we learn to love people?

Jesus tells us to love God supremely, and our neighbors as ourselves. If we cannot love ourselves or our neighbors, the problem may be that we do not love God. How can we love without God? God *is* love. (I John 4:16).

If the psychiatrists are correct, the primary problem of the mentally ill is lack of love for self. How do you love yourself?

How do you express love for your family and friends? Do you harp on their faults and failures? Of course not! You do your best to put them at ease and make them comfortable. What does it take to please you and make you comfortable? Are you happy with yourself when you fail to live up to your obligations? You don't dredge up your friends' faults, so why dwell on yours?

If you do not live within your means, what does that do to your self-respect? If you fail to carry your share of the load in your home, your church, or on your job, how can you feel good about yourself? Life is duty. Remember? Try doing your duty at home, in the community, and at work, and see what it does for your self-esteem.

The normal reaction to loss or pressure is depression. To lose status, position, family, or friends is depressing. (The most depressing thing about divorce is that it usually involves the loss of vital elements that make life worth living.) But any accumulation of minor pressures-

-responsibilities neglected, can produce major stress. Don't wallow in self-pity–go to work.

It is not necessarily the nature of one's work that contributes to self-esteem, but how well one performs that work. Ditch diggers and scrub women can sleep well, knowing they have made an essential contribution to the world. Everyone wants running water and clean homes, but few people want to dig ditches or scrub floors.

We are all prone to defend our egos by blaming others for our shortcomings. In doing so, we deceive no one but ourselves. That little maneuver does, however, put our associates on the defensive. And defensive people are certain to resent their position, and likely to strike out at anyone who puts them in that uncomfortable situation.

A blush is easily recognized as the physical manifestation of embarrassment, excitement, or anger. But what about nailbiting, allergies, ulcers, and countless other maladies?

The late Dr. John A. Schindler, Chairman of the Department of Medicine at the Monroe Clinic, Monroe, Wisconsin, said at least 50% of all physical ills were emotionally induced.

The late Dr. Otis Taylor, Jr. specialist in diagnosis and internal medicine, founder of the Taylor Clinic and Hospital, Lubbock, Texas, reported about 90% of his patients were victims of emotional stress.

Official statistics report half of all the hospital beds in America are filled with mental patients. Based on present statistics, authorities predict at least 1 out of every 10 Americans will be hospitalized for emotional illness, and they theorize that 1 out of 4 would profit from psychiatric treatment.

A psychological study conducted in an eastern state found 1 out of every 3 persons interviewed sufficiently emotionally disturbed to interfere with rational, productive living.

But these statistics involve people whose emotional problems are obvious. What about the physically ill patients whose illness is emotionally induced?

Several prominent psychiatrists agree that man has six basic psychological needs. They differ somewhat on the degree of importance, but all list love and security in the first and second place. Recognition, self-esteem, creative expression, and new experiences follow in random order.

When even one of these basic needs is unfulfilled, the person suffers emotional maladjustment, which may result in physical illness. Deprivation of several basic needs simultaneously usually results in an emotional breakdown.

According to Dr. Schindler, emotional stress may continue over a prolonged period of time before producing physical damage. However, brief trauma may result in a dangerous accident, and one severe emotional blow can immediately wreck one's physical function.

Dr. Schindler reported one patient, a strong healthy young father who collapsed completely when he went home from work and found his wife had killed herself and their only child. Three months later the man was still a complete vegetable.

Dr. Taylor said early in his practice, he suspected any illness of being emotionally induced unless he could see a fractured bone. Later he decided even broken bones were usually the result of emotional stress.

To his accident-prone patients, Dr. Taylor offered some free advice along with the casts and bandages: He insisted they check up on their emotional balance and stress tolerance

But suppose one has no one to love him, and no security? Would that not result in deprivation of the other four basic needs?

According to Dr. Schindler, it works about as well to give love and security as to get it (Jesus said it worked better).

For every lonely, unloved adult there are probably a dozen children in need of the love and guidance that adult could give. Children's Homes–both church and state–are usually begging for help.

There are hosts of helpless, lonely old people desperately in need of attention. In meeting their needs, the unloved, insecure adult can find love and security, and the other four basic needs will follow.

Solomon said, "A merry heart does good like a medicine, but a broken spirit dries up the bones" (Prov. 17:22). A broken spirit dehydrates more than bones. One of the many things it dries up is the bank account via medical bills. Then there are marriages and jobs. The emotionally ill are difficult to endure.

If one's sick emotions are not betrayed by nervous habits, allergies, or compulsive eating or drinking, they are sure to be revealed by psychological tests required by many employers. To exhibit a picture of health, one needs a happy frame of mind. What kind of picture does the world see when it looks at you?

Everyone wants to be happy; why is it so difficult?

Psychologists agree that a child is programmed to be happy or unhappy during the first year of life–especially the first three months.

For an adult to reprogram himself is not easy, but with adequate help it can be done–provided he is aware he needs to change and wants to do so.

It is difficult for an infant to relate to several people. This may account for the fact that the first and last children are usually more emotionally stable than the middle children in the family. They get more of Mother's attention.

Perhaps the new baby's need for a limited society was the reason the Creator arranged for his mother to feed him. Time was when infants thrived their first three months on an exclusive diet of mother's milk. That arrangement kept mother close by. And in that day ulcers and allergies in children were rare indeed. It is currently reported feeding infants food they cannot digest creates allergies.

The reason usually advanced by the atheist for his disbelief in God is that he cannot believe an all-wise, all-powerful, loving Creator would permit suffering and inequities in the world. The atheist ignores the fact that there was no suffering or inequity in the world until man disobeyed God. And he discounts how much misery could be wiped out even now by simple obedience to the Ten Commandments.

God said, "It is more blessed to give than to receive" (Acts 20:35). But how does man spend most of his time, talents, and energies? Getting, getting, and more getting! Is it strange he's so unhappy?

If giving brings happiness, what should one give, and to whom?

If love and security are the most basic needs, should one not start by supplying these at home?

If every American gave adequate love and security to his own family, what effect would it have on our burgeoning welfare program? Broken homes? Juvenile delinquency? And our annual 3 billion-dollar mental-hospital bill?

Children are prone to follow the example set by parents. When father and mother are kind to each other, and considerate of the other's welfare, children are likely to establish the same pattern of behavior toward parents, each other, and in the homes they establish.

When a child is deprived of love and security, he is prone to become selfish and self-centered. He is not likely to achieve constructive recognition or develop much self esteem. And the new experiences he encounters are not usually conducive to creative expression.

How can a child who grows up with a procession of babysitters feel loved or secure? If his own parents do not esteem him enough to give him their time, and attention, how can he feel of value?

It is impossible for a babysitter to provide much in the way of new experiences. Parents usually want their children to stay right where they leave them until they pick them up. And children in custodial care are generally forced to adhere to schedules that leave little room for creative expression.

Few Americans would deliberately maim their children emotionally. Why then are so many emotional cripples growing up in America?

Parents are so busy making money or seeking recreation that they fail to stop and ask themselves why they are doing what they are doing, or to evaluate the consequences.

How many people who grew up in material poverty really resent it? But note the bitterness of those who were emotionally deprived. It may be impossible for parents to provide material wealth for their children, and it is not correlated to happiness anyway. But all normal parents can provide love and affection, and that *is* essential to happiness.

A survey was made of 1000 successful men-not mere money makers, but men who blessed the world through their work.

Three hundred were farmers' sons; 200 started as newsboys; 100 were printers' apprentices; 100 began in factories; 50 started as common laborers on a railroad. Only 50 had wealthy parents to give them a start.

How many parents are depriving their children of true riches in an attempt to give them only things money can buy?

If love and security are the keys to happiness, should they not be provided to children at all costs? Can they be provided by babysitters, or hired help in institutions?

Shouldn't emotional cripples seek help as readily as the victims of broken bones? After all, emotional suffering is far more painful than a broken leg, and no more likely to heal without help.

The average American feels that emotional illness is a degrading, disgraceful, incurable malady to be concealed if at all possible. Actually, it is none of these things. It is the natural result of the deprivation of basic psychological needs-whether intentional or unintentional-and will disappear or recede when those needs are met.

And it is futile to attempt to hide the disease while one constantly flashes the symptoms.

The basic elements of depression, the Great American Plague, which afflicts some 35 million of us, are anger, guilt, lack of self-esteem, fear, and self-pity. The soil they grow in is isolation and idleness.

Depression victims, however, may insist they are not angry at anyone. But the most destructive anger is that which is directed toward oneself.

When we are angry with others, we can confront them or avoid them. But when we are angry with ourselves, confrontation is difficult, and avoidance impossible.

However, people who really do wrong rarely suffer as much guilt over it as the ones who fail to do the right things they know they ought to do.

Procrastination, for instance, produces anger, guilt, and fear. Then the procrastinator usually wallows in self-pity.

It is normal to be depressed when one suffers a painful loss: Death of a loved one, divorce, one's health, home, job, financial security, self-respect–the list of depressing situations is endless.

But any depression that lasts more than a month merits professional attention. It could be a malfunctioning thyroid, a viral illness, or whatever.

There has been a question for years as to the cause and effect of depression: Does depression cause a chemical imbalance in the body, or does a chemical imbalance cause depression? Recent research indicates each can generate the other, so medication may be necessary.

Victims of depression cannot control their feelings. They can, however, as long as they are still functional, control their actions. And if they discipline themselves to faithfully discharge their responsibilities, they will eventually find self-hatred giving way to self-respect.

Depression always produces sad, painful, destructive feelings. But several reputable psychologists contend negative feelings probably spawned the depression in the first place.

If negative feelings create depression (and there is no question depression produces negative feelings), then we have a vicious circle that must be broken before there can be any healing.

Dr. Tim La Haye, in his book *How to Win Over Depression* , offers encouragement and hope to anyone who is functional enough to follow his instructions. La Haye explains how to defeat depression–permanently. That is a better prognosis than the best psychiatrist can offer.

If depression is caused by fear, guilt, anger, and self-pity, why wouldn't eliminating those feelings cure the malady?

La Haye offers his key to defeating depression to anyone willing to use it. But if you do not have his book, the good doctor admits he "plagiarized" his entire philosophy from a book you **do** have: you can find the theme of his best-seller in Eph. 6:10-18 in your Bible.

So when you are depressed, get busy at useful work, and get involved with people. Cease your guilt-producing conduct, and you will probably find you are free from fear and anger; then you will not need to feel sorry for yourself.

If you cannot find enough work at home or on a job to keep busy (???), volunteer your services: Clean house for a sick friend, or mow a poor widow's lawn.

If you want to be depressed, look within. If you want to be defeated, look backwards. If you want to be distracted, look around you. But if you want to be delivered and delighted, look up.

The best place to find God is in a Bible-preaching, Bible-practicing church. You cannot be isolated there, and you can surely stay busy.

If your problem is spiritual, that must be solved before your physical and emotional symptoms will disappear. So what is the best way to solve our spiritual problems?

Chapter 17

HOW TO ACHIEVE SPIRITUAL ADEQUACY

How did the mighty Mississippi get to be the greatest river in America? Just one way: from the many tributaries that pour into its banks.

What are the tributaries that feed our spiritual lives? There are too many to possibly list in this study, but let's consider five primary ones: Christian fellowship, Public worship, Prayer, Bible study, and Witnessing.

You may not be able to attend public worship or read the Bible; and you may not know much about prayer or witnessing, but you can still enjoy Christian fellowship. It is the milk of the Word, as Bible study is the meat. Not everybody can eat meat, but the smallest infant can assimilate milk.

Fellowship

If you want to grow spiritually, associate with Christ-like people. Christianity is more caught than taught.

A Christian is like a brightly glowing coal in the fireplace. Remove it from the bed of coals and place it by itself on the hearth, and almost immediately it ceases to glow. Gradually it turns black and appears to be dead. But as soon as you return it to its place among the other coals. it begins to glow again.

John the Baptist, when he was shut up in prison, out of service, and away from the fellowship of other Christians, began to doubt the Lord (Luke 7:19).

Trying to be Christ-like apart from other Christians is like taking a sack lunch over in the corner by yourself, and saying, "I have all I need right here; I'll never go to the kitchen pantry, or grocery store again."

The Church is a fellowship of God's people. Without fellowship there is no church. And any time the fellowship is hurt, the church is damaged.

When you move to a new community where you have a choice of several churches, which one do you usually choose? The one with the most palatial building? The most eloquent preacher? The biggest crowds? The finest choir? The most comfortable pews? The best parking?

All those things may influence your choice a little, but none is the deciding factor. The reason given by the vast majority as to their preference of one church over another is, "The people were friendly." Sweet fellowship. That's what makes a church.

Public worship

The second tributary that contributes to Christian growth is public worship. Many insist public worship is dying. And it is true that social gospel preaching from modern pulpits, and social propaganda from church literature has practically emptied the churches of many denominations. But where preachers still preach "Jesus saves" -not socialism, and teachers still teach the Bible, congregations are alive and growing.

As a rule, Christians grow in the grace and power of God in direct proportion to their faithfulness in public worship (Psa. 92:13).

Many professing Christians refuse to attend church because "there are so many hypocrites" there. It's strange that the presence of hypocrites never prevents their attending ball games, movies, school functions, or anything except church.

The Bible commands us not to forsake the assembling of ourselves together (Heb. 10:2425), and Jesus set the example of faithfulness in attendance at God's house (Luke 4:16). Read up on the conditions at that time, and see if you don't agree that hypocrisy was far more prevalent then than now.

Abraham was called the father of the faithful. When you read the accounts of his wanderings, notice that every time he made camp, he built an altar unto the Lord and worshipped there. He did not wait until he got settled to get back to worship service.

We know that God's presence fills the universe; He certainly could not be confined to earth, or to any one house on the earth. Yet it is His plan to have a house in each community where His people can gather for fellowship and worship. And He has promised to meet them there (Deut.

12:5-14; I Kings 8:26-30; Ezra 5:15; 6:7; Neh. 13:11; Isa. 2:3; I Peter 4:17).

God did not command us to worship in His house–provided we enjoy the preaching, and the music, or that the pews are comfortable and the temperature pleasing; He said come to His house and bring an offering. And Micah tells us the offering the Lord wants most is an humble and contrite heart (Micah 6:6-8).

God also promised to give us pastors to feed the flock with knowledge and understanding (Jer 3:15). If the pastor is not feeding the flock, it is probably because the people chose him–not God (Jer. 5:31). What then? God says stand up and ask that the pastors return to God's ways. If we don't ask, or if the pastors refuse, God promises to punish the guilty (Jer. 6:13-19), but He still did not direct us to avoid public worship.

If the fellowship and worship is not what we think it ought to be, we are commanded to call on the Lord to straighten it out (Zech. 13:7-9). God holds the shepherds in His hand (Rev. 1:12-20). Disciplining the pastor is His job–not ours.

Prayer

The third major tributary to the river of spirituality is prayer.

But you say, "I don't really know how to pray."

Join the crowd! How many of us know as much about prayer as we need to know? The earliest disciples felt the same (Luke 11:1).

Jesus did not rebuke His followers for their ignorance; he taught them. But how ironic that He admonished His listeners just before He gave them the model prayer that they should not use vain repetitions like the heathen; and that same model prayer has been made into a vain repetition.

A veteran cafe man said he always gave a free meal to any indigent, bum, or wino, the first time he asked–provided he could repeat the "Lord's Prayer." He said nine out of ten of them could do it.

Anyone who follows the teachings in that wonderful model prayer would never need to beg (Psa. 37:25). There is no virtue, however, in merely being able to repeat it without understanding it, or abiding by its precepts.

What is prayer? It is communication with God. It does not need to be a flowery speech. Probably our most profitable prayers are little more than the sincere desires of our hearts turned heavenward.

Note the prayers of great men of faith in the Bible. When Moses felt he could go no further, and the people were angry enough to kill him, he cried out to God, "What shall I do unto this people? they be almost ready to stone me" (Ex. 17:4).

Doesn't sound like much of a prayer, does it? But it got results. God told Moses what to do; he did it, and God provided water for the thirst-crazed people.

When David was fleeing for his life from the hand of Saul, he almost got cornered at Keilah, where he had just saved the city from the Philistines. He asked God, "Will the men of Keilah deliver me up?" God said, "They will deliver you up." So David fled to safety.

We don't need to tell God all about our troubles; He already knows more about them than we do. And above all things, we should not tell Him *how* to solve our problems; He has far better solutions than we could possibly imagine.

The example Jesus gave us in prayer has three parts: praise, intercession, and petition. And notice that it begins and ends with praise. Reverence and gratitude are vital ingredients of prayer.

Paul said we were to be thankful for all things (Eph. 5:20). We never know when something that seems to be an unbearable curse at the time, may turn out to be a blessing. Being beaten and thrown in jail didn't look much like a blessing to Paul and Silas. But they praised God anyway, and out of that experience came the conversion of the Philippian jailer, and a strong church at Philippi.

After praying for fifteen years to go to Rome, Paul was probably not overjoyed at going as a prisoner in chains. But he praised God, and went on. How else would he have managed to get free passage, an armed guard, and an invitation to speak in Caesar's palace?

There are many fringe benefits to prayer. When we pray for our friends (or enemies), God always shows us something we can do to improve the situation. (Perhaps that's one reason we do so little praying; we don't want to do any work.)

When we pray for others and their needs, we can't forget about them. Haven't you had the best intentions of doing something for sick or troubled friends-but you forgot. The most important thing you forgot was to pray for them.

If we pray for people, we can't hate them. We can't ask God to forgive *us* , and refuse to hold a forgiving spirit toward others.

We can't seek God's guidance in choosing a vocation, a location, or a mate-and then make a choice we *know* is contrary to God's word.

If we pray for God's protection on a journey, we have to be careful to obey the traffic rules, drive defensively, and show kindness and courtesy to others. If we ask God to go with us through the day, we can't afford to go somewhere He would not want to go.

Before we pray, it is good to remind ourselves that God will not do anything for us we can do for ourselves. If there is any way we could do it ourselves, we should not ask God to do it for us. And it is useless to ask God to do what you want Him to do for you, unless you are willing to do what He wants you to do for Him (Zech. 7:13).

How can you know what to ask God for?

It doesn't matter–as long as you ask according to His will. He won't give it to you anyway if it isn't good for you. Would you give your little child a sharp razor just because he asked for it?

But how can you know if it's God's will?

That's where Bible study comes in.

Bible study

To learn God's Word you should familiarize yourself with the entire Bible. And that is difficult to do with one reading. Next you should study it by books, then by topics, and whatever other method seems to best meet your needs.

When you are properly acquainted with your Bible, it is simple to check and see what God has to say about any subject before you contemplate a course of action or pray about it. Most of your questions can be answered by refreshing your memory with Ex. 20, Matt. 6:33, and 7:12.

If just the Christians in America would read the Bible, and obey God's commandments, half the doctors, lawyers, psychiatrists, and pharmacists would have to change their professions.

What does the Bible say you should do about your most pressing problem? Do it, and see if God doesn't take care of the situation–even if it takes a miracle. When we do the right thing, God has promised to bless us (John 15:7; Rom. 8:28).

According to modern philosophers and many social-gospel preachers, however, there is no right or wrong; everything is relative. One should do as the situation dictates.

But God says "There is a way which seems right to a man, but the end thereof is the way of death" (Prov. 14:12). And after all, God is to be our judge at the final judgment.

Paul said to the young preacher, Timothy, "Study to show yourself approved into God, a workman who need not be ashamed, rightly dividing the Word of truth."

If preachers do not study the Bible, they will have double cause to be ashamed, because they will not be able to "rightly divide" or explain the meaning of the Scriptures to their congregations. Pastors can't very well "feed the sheep" unless they possess more knowledge than their hearers. Knowledge does not come without study. And no collection of books can adequately substitute for the Bible.

Bible study is probably the biggest tributary that contributes to our spirituality. And don't be misled by the common fallacy that an ordinary layman cannot understand the Bible. Anyone can understand the Bible who has the Holy Spirit for a teacher (John 14:26, 16:13).

When you begin to study the Bible (after you have read it enough to become familiar with it), ask yourself three questions as you consider each passage: Who said it? To whom was he speaking? What was the purpose of the message?

By taking a passage out of context or misapplying it, one can prove almost anything

Page 136

by the Bible. Remember "Judas went out and hanged himself. . .Go thou and do likewise. . .And what thou doest, do quickly. . ." That's all Scripture if you don't mind twisting it around a little.

Anyone who was reared in a Christian home, or attended church and Sunday School probably already had strong convictions about what the Bible taught long before he could read it for himself. The average person reads the Bible–not to find out what it teaches, but to prove what he already believes.

Jesus Himself said, "Seek, and you shall find. . ." So be careful in studying the Scriptures that you are seeking God's truth, and His will for your life–not to prove what you already believe, or an excuse to do what you have already determined to do.

Bible study is like manna from heaven: We need to seek it every day. If we try to store it, like the manna, it loses its value.

God described Job as a perfect and upright man. Job said that he obeyed God's commandments, and that he preferred the Word of God (food for his soul) to food for his body (Job 23:12).

How many Christians had rather read their Bibles than eat?

Witnessing

The fifth and final great tributary of spirituality is witnessing. What exercise is to the body, witnessing is to the soul. The more of the love of God you share with others, the more you have to keep for yourself.

Jesus said, "You shall be witnesses unto me. . ." He did not say, "You ought to be" but "You *shall* be witnesses. . ." So if you are a Christian, you are a witness for Christ. The big question is, what kind of witness are you?

When low-hovering clouds shroud the supports of San Francisco's famed Golden Gate Bridge, it appears to be suspended in mid air with no means of support. Motorists who know, however, that adequate steel girders lie hidden in the mists and fog drive on unafraid, and others follow in their train.

Human eye cannot see the power of God that holds the Universe in space; we have to take His Word for it.

Relatively few people saw the risen Christ after he emerged from the tomb, or heard His promise to go and prepare a place for us; but multiplied millions have accepted the witness of those who did. What has that witness meant to your life? Do you want to share it?

Witnessing is not, as some people think, tucking a Bible under your arm, knocking on doors, and telling strangers that God loves them. If they have normal intelligence, they already know that.

Jesus said, "As my Father has sent me, even so send I you" (John 20:21). When John the Baptist questioned that Jesus was the Christ, Jesus told the disciples to go tell John what they had seen and heard of His ministry: The blind had been made to see, the lame to walk, the lepers cleansed, deaf ears opened, the dead raised, and the gospel preached to the poor (Matt. 11:2-6).

The answer Jesus gave His disciples is the key to what witnessing really is. If you help to maintain churches or missions where the gospel is preached, you are witnessing. Financing the colleges, seminaries, and Bible institutes that train workers for God's kingdom is witnessing.

When the gospel is preached, people will be saved. Every soul that is saved is raised from the dead (Eph. 2:1-7). So any time you have any part in winning a soul to faith in Jesus Christ, you are raising the dead. This is witnessing in its finest form.

But there are many ways to win people to faith in Christ besides preaching to them. One way is ministering to them when they are ill. If you support hospitals that heal in the name of the Lord-with or without charge, you are witnessing.

Jesus said His followers should do the works that He did, and even greater works than He did, after the Holy Spirit came to help them (John 14:12). That statement has mystified many Christians. But what Jesus said is always true.

A veteran missionary to Africa said that was one Scripture she could never understand until she reached her mission station. She said of her work there, "I have healed more sick bodies with salt water than Jesus ever healed during His entire earthly ministry."

Merely providing the money for others to teach, preach, and heal in the name of the Lord is not all of witnessing, however. Micah really summed it up when he said, "What does the Lord require of you but to do justly, love mercy, and walk humbly with your God" (Micah 6:8).

Any time a Christian treats his neighbor unjustly, he has denied the Lord who saved him. (And not paying your debts or supporting yourself and dependents is treating your neighbor unjustly-specifically, it's stealing from him.) That is witnessing, however; it is saying you do not believe God's Word, and you do not fear His judgment. If Christians do not believe or fear God, how can they possibly expect others to do so?

When a Christian suffers mistreatment rather than disobey God, he is saying he had rather please God than himself. And he is showing love for his neighbor by proving he had rather be hurt than to hurt others.

Jesus said the greatest commandment was to love God supremely and your neighbor as yourself (Matt. 22:36-39). He also said, "If you love me, keep my commandments" (John 14:15). So the best witnessing any Christian can do is to cheerfully keep the commandments.

"Why won't you come to church?" a pastor asked the husband of one of his new members. The preacher had observed that the young man possessed more Christlike qualities than the majority of his congregation.

"My wife goes every Sunday," the young man replied. "It has not improved her one bit. She comes home just as cross and ill-tempered with the children and me as she was before she went. She still doesn't cook, keep house, or make any effort to make a comfortable, happy home for us. I can't see that Christianity has helped her, so why should I try it?"

How different that woman's testimony from that of a new convert in India. When asked what she did when her husband beat her, she said, "I clean his house and cook him a good meal. And when he curses me, I tell him that God and I love him."

Do you reverence God's Word, His name, His house, and His day? If you don't, you are witnessing to the fact that you do not love Him.

Do you show concern for your neighbor's welfare? If so, you have to be concerned about his soul. That's the most important part of his welfare.

Your closest neighbors, of course, are your mate, your children, and your parents. Do you love them? Do you show your love by being kind and patient, and doing your best to make them comfortable, and happy?

And what about your neighbor next door, or the new one down the street. Does he know God? If so, does he have a church home where he attends regularly? Do you live before your family, friends, and neighbors in such a way that it does not embarrass you to invite them to church, or talk to them about God and the welfare of their souls?

It is as impossible to be strong spiritually without Christian fellowship, public worship, prayer, Bible study, and witnessing as it is to be strong physically without food, drink, and exercise.

Are you satisfied with your spiritual condition? Do you want spiritual power? All you have to do is meet God's conditions, and ask for it (Luke 11:13).

How many miracles would you like to have? Do you need them to glorify God-or for your own pleasure?

Some people want to be used of God, but too many merely want to *use Him.*

God created man for *His* pleasure-not ours. Anyone who wants to be an instrument of God's righteousness (Rom. 6:13) will find life exciting, joyous, and fulfilling.

Anyone who tries to use God, however, will encounter an endless round of frustration, disappointment, and misery.

God will not be used of anybody. The suicide is usually a person who feels God has failed Him. What probably happened is that God refused to be manipulated by a weak and foolish human being.

A Texas man sued a church for $800 he claimed to have paid in tithes. He said the pastor promised him he would get rich if he tithed. He tried it; it didn't work, so he asked for his money back. (An anonymous donor sent $800 to the church to pay the disgruntled "tither.")

God never promised to make anybody rich provided he tithed. And it is doubtful if any preacher ever said so. God promised to give more blessings than they were able to receive to *His children* who tithed. He is a much better judge than we are of what we are able to receive (Mal. 3:10). Money in not always a blessing; it often brings more pain than pleasure. True wealth is happiness, love, peace of mind, and serenity-not money. God promises abundant blessings to His children who tithe, and He always keeps His promises.

Are you sure the miracles you want would glorify God and promote His kingdom? If so, you can be sure He wants you to have them.

Remember that Jesus taught us to begin and end our prayers with praise. Have you sincerely expressed gratitude to God for the blessings He has already given you? Ingratitude is a most despised sin in God's eyes (Isa. 1:2-4). Why should God shower more blessings upon us if we are not grateful for the ones He has already given us?

The shortest path from depression to elation is counting your blessings. In case you think you have no blessings to count, imagine what it would be like if you lost everything you have: family, friends, food, shelter, and health-

including sight and hearing. Then, like Job, suppose you got it all back?

After evaluating that situation, search your heart for motives (James 4:3), and God's Word for directions (Prov. 3:6); when the two are in tune you can expect more blessings than you have room to receive.

*"Families who worship
and pray together,
stay together."*

THE CONCLUSION

After evaluating the facts, do you really think there are any authentic grounds for blaming God for your personal problems or the chaos in the world?

If two people sit down at a piano and one gets nothing but discord from the keys, while the other brings forth haunting melodies, does anyone blame the piano for the discord?

Life is much like a piano. The harmony is there--and the cacophony. Anyone who learns to play it correctly can bring forth beauty. Play it contrary to the rules, and it gives nothing but ugliness. God is not at fault.

If you were told to go into a supermarket and choose whatever you wanted to give you health, happiness, and pleasure, would you choose poisonous food and drink? Isn't it just as foolish in the storehouse of life to poison our bodies with nicotine, alcohol, and narcotics; and our emotions with hate, selfishness, resentment, anger, and jealousy?

If you do make such choices, is God to blame? It's true He made you a creature of free will, but would you want to be otherwise?

Our Creator has provided minute and specific instructions to guide us to happy, fruitful, victorious lives. If we neglect to read or fail to heed His instructions, have we any right to blame Him when things go wrong?

"When all else fails, read directions." They are ample and specific from Genesis to the Revelation.